# TEACHER'S PET PUBLICATIONS

LITPLAN TEACHER PACK
for
Narrative of the Life of Frederick Douglass
based on the autobiography by
Frederick Douglass

Written by
Barbara M. Linde, MA Ed.

TABLE OF CONTENTS
Narrative of the Life of Frederick Douglass

ABOUT THE AUTHOR

Frederick Douglass

DOUGLASS, Frederick (approximately 1818-1895) Frederick Douglass is thought to have been born in February, 1818 on Holmes Hill Farm in Easton, Maryland. Since Douglass was born into slavery, and slave births were not recorded, there is no accurate verification of his date of birth. His mother, Harriet Baily, was a slave on the Holmes Hill Farm. She gave her son the name Frederick Augustus Washington Bailey. His father was white, and one possibility is that the owner of the farm, Aaron Anthony, was his father.

As a young child, Frederick lived with his grandmother, Betsy Bailey, a short distance from the Holmes Hill Farm. When he was six she had to take him to live with his siblings on the Lloyd Plantation, which was also managed by Aaron Anthony. He rarely had enough to eat and had only meager clothing. His mother died when he was seven, although he did not find this out until much later.

When he was eight, he was sent to live in Baltimore with Hugh Auld, the brother-in-law of Lucretia Auld, who was Aaron Anthony's daughter. In his new home, Frederick was well treated. He ran errands and cared for the family's two-year-old. Sophia Auld, Hugh's wife, taught Frederick how to read and write. When Hugh found out he made her stop, but Frederick continued learning on his own. He realized that knowledge was the key to freedom.

At age fifteen Frederick was once again sent to the fields to work. He was considered to be difficult to handle and was sent to a slave breaker. When he was eighteen he was returned to Hugh Auld in Baltimore and was trained to be a ship caulker. He made one unsuccessful attempt to escape. On September 3, 1838, Anna Murray, a free black woman and his fiancee, helped him with his successful escape. He disguised himself as a free sailor and took a train from Baltimore to Philadelphia, then transferred to a train going to New York. Once there, he took the surname Johnson.

A few days after he arrived in New York, Murray joined him and they were married. They moved to New Bedford, Massachusetts. There he took the surname Douglass. In 1839 he began reading the abolitionist newspaper Liberator. In 1841 he met the publisher, William Lloyd Garrison. By then Douglass was also giving speeches to white abolitionists and the Massachusetts Anti-Slavery Society hired him as a traveling speaker. From 1839 until 1844 he and Anna also had four children.

Some people did not believe that Douglass had been a slave, because his speech and manner gave the impression that he was well-educated. The Massachusetts Anti-Slavery Society suggested that he write his autobiography, which he did in the winter of 1844-1845. The book became a best seller and received positive critical reviews. Also because of the popularity of the book, Douglass found his life and freedom in jeopardy. He left the country and spent the next two years lecturing in England, Scotland, and Ireland. In December 1846 Ellen and Anna Richardson of Newcastle, England paid Hugh Auld seven hundred dollars for Douglass's freedom.

Douglass returned from England and began a career as a journalist and publisher. He died in Washington, D. C. on February 20, 1895. His body lay in state in Washington and then was buried in Rochester, New York.

INTRODUCTION *Narrative of the Life of Frederick Douglass*

This unit has been designed to develop students' reading, writing, thinking, listening, and speaking skills through exercises and activities related to *Narrative of the Life of Frederick Douglass, an American Slave* by Frederick Douglass. It includes twenty lessons, supported by extra resource materials.

The **introductory lesson** introduces students to *Narrative of the Life of Frederick Douglass, an American Slave*. Following the introductory activity, students are given an explanation of how the activity relates to the book they are about to read. Following the transition, students are given the materials they will be using during the unit. They are also introduced to the non-fiction assignment. At the end of the lesson, students begin the pre-reading work for the first reading assignment.

The **reading assignments** are approximately 30 pages each; some are a little shorter while others are a little longer. Students have approximately 15 minutes of pre-reading work to do prior to each reading assignment. This pre-reading work involves reviewing the study questions for the assignment and doing some vocabulary work for 8 to 10 vocabulary words they will encounter in their reading.

The **study guide questions** are fact-based questions; students can find the answers to these questions right in the text. These questions come in two formats: short answer or multiple choice. The best use of these materials is probably to use the short answer version of the questions as study guides for students (since answers will be more complete), and to use the multiple-choice version for occasional quizzes. It might be a good idea to make transparencies of your answer keys for the overhead projector.

The **vocabulary work** is intended to enrich students' vocabularies as well as to aid in the students' understanding of the book. Prior to each reading assignment, students will complete a two-part worksheet for approximately 8 to 10 vocabulary words in the upcoming reading assignment. Part I focuses on students' use of general knowledge and contextual clues by giving the sentence in which the word appears in the text. Students are then to write down what they think the words mean based on the words' usage. Part II gives students dictionary definitions of the words and has them match the words to the correct definitions based on the words' contextual usage. Students should then have an understanding of the words when they meet them in the text.

After each reading assignment, students will go back and formulate answers for the study guide questions. Discussion of these questions serves as a review of the most important events and ideas presented in the reading assignments.

After students complete extra discussion questions, there is a vocabulary review lesson which pulls together all of the separate vocabulary lists for the reading assignments and gives students a review of all of the words they have studied.

Following the reading of the book, a lesson is devoted to the extra discussion questions/writing assignments. These questions focus on interpretation, critical analysis, and personal response, employing a variety of thinking skills and adding to the students' understanding of the novel. These questions are done as a **group activity**.

Using the information they have acquired so far through individual work and class discussions, students get together to further examine the text and to brainstorm ideas relating to the themes of the novel.

The group activity is followed by a **reports and discussion** session in which the groups share their ideas about the book with the entire class; thus, the entire class gets exposed to many different ideas regarding the themes and events of the book.

There are **three writing assignments** in this unit, each with the purpose of informing, persuading, or having students express personal opinions. The first assignment is to **inform**. Students will write an autobiographical sketch modeled after Douglass's autobiography. The second writing assignment is to **persuade**. Students will write a speech relating to a topic about which they feel passionate. The third writing assignment is to **express a personal opinion.** Students will explain how well they think the autobiography does what Douglass said he had hoped it would do.

In addition, there is a **non-fiction reading assignment**. Students are required to read a piece of non-fiction related in some way to *Narrative of the Life of Frederick Douglass, an American Slave*. After reading their non-fiction pieces, students will fill out a worksheet on which they answer questions regarding facts, interpretation, criticism, and personal opinions. During one class period, students make oral presentations about the non-fiction pieces they have read. This not only exposes all students to a wealth of information; it also gives students the opportunity to practice public speaking.

The **review lesson** pulls together all of the aspects of the unit. The teacher is given four or five choices of activities or games to use which all serve the same basic function of reviewing all of the information presented in the unit.

The **unit test** comes in two formats: multiple choice or short answer. As a convenience, two different tests for each format have been included. There is also an advanced short answer unit test for advanced students.

There are additional **support materials** included with this unit. The **resource materials sections** include suggestions for an in-class library, crossword and word search puzzles related to the novel, and extra vocabulary worksheets. There is a list of **bulletin board ideas** which gives the teacher suggestions for bulletin boards to go along with this unit. In addition, there is a list of extra class activities the teacher could choose from to enhance the unit or as a substitution for an exercise the teacher might feel is inappropriate for his/her class. Answer keys are located directly after the reproducible student materials throughout the unit.

Note: Some editions of the book contain an Introduction, Notes on the Text, a Preface, additional Letters, and an Appendix. These sections are not treated in this Lit Plan. It is up to the discretion of the individual teacher whether or not to use these sections.

ADAPTATIONS:
Block Schedule
1. Depending on the length of your class periods, and the frequency with which the class meets, you may wish to choose one of the following options:

2. Complete two of the daily lessons in one class period.

3. Have students complete all reading and writing activities in class.

4. Assign all reading to be completed out of class, and concentrate on the worksheets and discussions in class.

5. Assign the projects from the daily lessons at the beginning of the unit, and allow time each day

for students to work on them.

6. Use some of the Unit and Vocabulary Resource activities during every class.

Gifted & Talented / Advanced Classes

1. Emphasize the projects and the extra discussion questions.

2. Have students complete all of the writing activities.

3. Assign the reading to be completed out of class and focus on the discussions in class.

4. Encourage students to develop their own questions.

ELL Students / ELD

1. Assign a partner to help the student read the text aloud.

2. Tape record the text and have the student listen and follow along in the text.

3. Give the student the study guide worksheets to use as they read.

4. Provide pictures and demonstrations to explain difficult vocabulary words and concepts.

5. Conduct guided reading lessons, asking students to stop frequently and explain what they have read.

6. Show the movie version of the novel and help students identify characters and events, and relate the action in their own words. You may want to show the movie without the sound and explain the actions in your own words.

UNIT OBJECTIVES *Narrative of the Life of Frederick Douglass*

1. Through reading *Narrative of the Life of Frederick Douglass, an American Slave*, students will analyze characters and their situations to better understand the themes of the autobiography.

2. Students will understand and describe the characteristics of an autobiography.

3. Students will demonstrate their understanding of the text on four levels: factual, interpretive, critical, and personal.

4. Students will be able to identify cause and effect situations in the autobiography.

5. Students will be able to identify and discuss the tone of the autobiography.

6. Students will practice reading aloud and silently to improve their skills in each area.

7. Students will enrich their vocabularies and improve their understanding of the novel through the vocabulary lessons prepared for use in conjunction with it.

8. Students will answer questions to demonstrate their knowledge and understanding of the main events and characters in *Narrative of the Life of Frederick Douglass, an American Slave*.

9. Students will practice writing through a variety of writing assignments. The writing assignments in this are geared to several purposes:

    a. To check the students' reading comprehension

    b. To make students think about the ideas presented by the autobiography

    c. To make students put those ideas into perspective

    d. To encourage critical and logical thinking

    e. To provide the opportunity to practice good grammar and improve students' use of the English language.

10. Students will read aloud, report, and participate in large and small group discussions to improve their public speaking and personal interaction skills.

Date Assigned	Assignment	Completion Date
	Assignment 1 Chapters I-III	
	Assignment 2 Chapters IV-VI	
	Assignment 3 Chapters VII-IX	
	Assignment 4 Chapter X	
	Assignment 5 Chapters XI, Appendix	

UNIT OUTLINE *Narrative of the Life of Frederick Douglass*

1 Introduction	2 Nonfiction Assignment	3 PVR Chapters I-III Minilesson: Autobiography	4 Study ?s I-III Writing Assignment #1	5 PVR Chapters IV-VI Oral REading Evaluation
6 Study ?s IV-VI	7 Quiz I-VI Writing Conferences PVR VII-IX	8 Study?s VII-IX Minilesson:Tone PVR X	9 Video	10 Study ?s X Minilesson: Cause and Effect
11 Writing Assignment #2	12 PVR XI-Appendix	13 Library for Independent Work	14 Extra Discussion Questions	15 Quotations
16 Writing Assignment #3	17 Vocabulary Review	18 Unit Review	19 Unit Test	20 Nonfiction Assignment

Key: P = Preview Study Questions   V = Vocabulary Work   R = Read

STUDY GUIDE QUESTIONS

Assignment 1
Chapters I-III

1. Where and when was Frederick Douglass born? What was his name at birth? What did he know about his parents?

2. How old was Frederick Douglass when he wrote his narrative?

3. Describe Frederick's relationship with his mother. Include the number of times they saw each other, what their visits were like, and Frederick's age when she died.

4. What are Douglass's observations about the mulatto children--those who had a slave mother but a white father, who was usually the slave owner?

5. What are Douglass's observations about this class of mulatto slaves in relation to the south and the American idea of the correctness of slavery?

6. Who was Douglass's first master? Also name the members of his family. Tell where they lived.

7. Describe the slaves' monthly allowance of food and yearly clothing. Describe their beds and bedding.

8. What did Douglass say about the singing of the slaves? How did he feel about the songs?

9. Describe Colonel Lloyd's method for keeping slaves out of his garden.

10. Summarize Douglass's observations about the reasons the slaves usually gave only positive, complimentary comments about their masters.

Assignment 2
Chapters IV-VI

1. Douglass says that Mr. Gore was "cruel, artful, and obdurate." What are the examples that Douglass gives for each of these adjectives about Mr. Gore?

2. What did Mr. Gore do to the slave named Demby? Why did he do this? What punishment did Mr. Gore receive? Why?

3. Who were Mr. Thomas Lanman, Mrs. Hick, and Mr. Beal Bondy? What did each of them do? What were the results of their actions?

4. How did Master Daniel Lloyd treat the young Douglass?

5. How old was Douglass when he left the Lloyd plantation? Where did he go? With whom did he live there? What was his job?

6. What did Douglass think about his departure from Colonel Lloyd's plantation?

7. To what did Douglass attribute his good fortune?

8. What did Mrs. Auld teach Douglass to do? What did Mr. Auld say when he found out?

9. What did Douglass think about Mr. Auld's comments? What did Douglass decide to do in light of the comments?

10. Compare and contrast the treatment of slaves by the slave owners in the city with the slave owners on the plantations.

Assignment 3

Chapters VII-IX

1. How did Mrs. Auld change during the time that Douglass lived with the Auld family? What made her change?

2. How did Douglass learn to read?

3. How old was Douglass when he read "*The Columbian Orator*"? What effect did this book have on him?

4. Why did Douglass say that learning to read was a curse instead of a blessing?

5. What word did Douglass hear that was of interest to him? How did he find out the meaning? Why was this word interesting?

6. Describe how Douglass learned to write.

7. What event happened about three years after Douglass began living in Baltimore that again reminded him that he detested slavery?

8. What regret did Douglass express about the time when he was moved from Master Hugh's home to Master Thomas? Why did he have this regret?

9. Douglass says that Master Thomas was a mean man. Which of Thomas's practices was considered the meanest, even among slaveholders?

10. Where did Master Thomas send Douglass, for how long, and why?

Assignment 4

Chapter X

1. What happened to Douglass almost every week for the first six months that he lived with Covey?

2. Douglass says that he was "somewhat unmanageable" when he first went to live with Covey. How does Douglass describe himself after he had been with Covey for a few months?

3. Summarize Douglass's thoughts when he looked at the ships on the Chesapeake Bay.

4. What did Covey do to Douglass when he (Douglass) became sick while fanning the wheat?

5. What did Douglass do as a result of Covey's treatment of him? What was the result of Douglass's actions? What did Douglass do?

6. What suggestion did another slave named Sandy Jenkins give to Douglass? What did Douglass do?

7. Describe the turning point in Douglass's life as a slave that happened when he was with Covey.

8. According to Douglass, what institution is the "mere covering for the most horrid crimes"? What type of slaveholders are the worst? Why does Douglass think this?

9. Describe Douglass's first attempt to run away. Tell who was with him, what the plan was, how far they got in the attempt, and what happened to each of the men after they were caught.

10. What trade did Douglass learn? What was his situation at the end of a year of working at this trade? What was unfair about this situation?

Assignment 5

<u>Chapters XI, Appendix</u>

1. Why didn't Douglass give all of the details of his escape?

2. How did Douglass feel about the underground railroad?

3. Master Hugh sometimes gave Douglass six cents of his wages after he had made six dollars, supposedly to encourage him. What effect did this have on Douglass?

4. Why did Douglass want to hire himself out, even though Master Hugh took most of the wages?

5. When did Douglass succeed in escaping? Where did he go? How did Douglass feel when he arrived in the free state?

6. What motto did Douglass adopt in the free state. Why?

7. Who helped Douglass and what were some of the results of his help?

8. Describe how Frederick Bailey took the name of Douglass. Include all of the names he used, including the name his mother gave him.

9. What newspaper did Douglass begin to read? How did this newspaper affect his ideas and actions?

10. Summarize Douglass's thoughts on the type of Christianity that he calls the slaveholding religion.

Assignment 1

Chapters I-III

1. Where and when was Frederick Douglass born? What was his name at birth? What did he know about his parents?

   He was born in Tuckahoe, near Hillsboro, Maryland. He did not know when he was born but estimated that it was around 1818. His name was Frederick Augustus Washington Bailey. His mother was a slave named Harriet Bailey. He believed that his father was a white man named Captain Aaron Anthony, who owned Harriet Bailey.

2. How old was Frederick Douglass when he wrote his narrative?

   He was about twenty-seven or twenty-eight.

3. Describe Frederick's relationship with his mother. Include the number of times they saw each other, what their visits were like, and Frederick's age when she died.

   Frederick was taken from his mother when he was less than a year old and was then raised by his grandmother. His mother was sent to a farm about twelve miles away to work. He only saw her four or five times in his life. On those occasions, she walked after her workday to the farm where he lived. She put him to bed and then left. She died when he was seven, but he was not permitted to be with her when she was sick or when she died.

4. What are Douglass's observations about the mulatto children--those who had a slave mother but a white father, who was usually the slave owner?

   The law said that the children of slave women would always become slaves. The slave owner's wife was offended by the presence of the mulatto children. The children were often sold off so the father would not have to either whip them himself or witness their beatings by his wife or white sons.

5. What are Douglass's observations about this class of mulatto slaves in relation to the south and the American idea of the correctness of slavery?

   Douglass observed that these slaves looked very different from the original African slaves and from the white southerners. He thought their presence might do away with the reasoning that since God cursed Ham, then American slavery was right. Since so many of the slaves were of mixed blood, the reasoning that the descendants of Ham should be cursed would no longer apply.

6. Who was Douglass's first master? Also name the members of his family. Tell where they lived.

   His first master was called Captain Anthony. He had two sons named Andrew and Richard, a daughter, Lucretia, and her husband, Thomas Auld. They all lived in a house on the plantation of Colonel Edward Lloyd. Anthony was Lloyd's clerk.

7. Describe the slaves' monthly allowance of food and yearly clothing. Describe their beds and bedding.

   Each month, the adult men and women slaves received eight pounds of pork or fish and one bushel of corn meal. Each year they got two coarse linen shirts, one pair of linen trousers, one jacket, one pair of trousers for winter, one pair of shoes, and one pair of stockings. The children's allowance was given to their mother or the woman who was raising them. Young children who did not work had only two linen shirts per year. Most of the children under age 10 went naked. They slept on the floor with only thin blankets.

8. What did Douglass say about the singing of the slaves? How did he feel about the songs?
It was a common belief that slaves sang because they were happy, but this was not true. He said the slaves sang the most when they were unhappy. The songs were a testimony against slavery. Douglass was not able to hear the songs without thinking about the dehumanizing aspects of slavery.

9. Describe Colonel Lloyd's method for keeping slaves out of his garden.
He spread tar on the fence around the garden. If a slave was caught with tar on his person, it was proof that the slave had tried to get in the garden, or had been in the garden. The slave was punished.

10. Summarize Douglass's observations about the reasons the slaves usually gave only positive, complimentary comments about their masters.
The masters had spies among the slaves, and if it was reported that a slave said negative things, the slave could be sold off. Slaves also thought of their own situation as better than that of other slaves. They also thought the greatness of their masters transferred to them.

Assignment 2
Chapters IV-VI

1. Douglass says that Mr. Gore was "cruel, artful, and obdurate." What are the examples that Douglass gives for each of these adjectives about Mr. Gore?
He was cruel enough to inflict the most severe punishment. He was artful enough to be very tricky. He was obdurate enough to ignore his conscience.

2. What did Mr. Gore do to the slave named Demby? Why did he do this? What punishment did Mr. Gore receive? Why?
Mr. Gore shot and killed Demby when Demby refused to come out of the creek where he had taken refuge from a beating. Gore said that if even one slave could be allowed to get away without being corrected, the others would not listen, and then they would all get their freedom. Gore was not punished because the slave owners agreed with him. Also, the only witnesses to the murder were slaves, and the slaves could not sue a white man or testify against him.

3. Who were Mr. Thomas Lanman, Mrs. Hick, and Mr. Beal Bondy? What did each of them do? What were the results of their actions?
They were all white slave owners who killed slaves. None of them were convicted since it was not a crime to kill a slave or any other colored person.

4. How did Master Daniel Lloyd treat the young Douglass?
Lloyd protected Frederick from the older boys and shared food with him.

5. How old was Douglass when he left the Lloyd plantation? Where did he go? With whom did he live there? What was his job?
He was about seven or eight when he was sent to Baltimore to live with Mr. Hugh Auld and his family. He was to take care of the Aulds' young son, Thomas.

6. What did Douglass think about his departure from Colonel Lloyd's plantation?
He thought it was one of the most interesting events of his life. Going to Baltimore was the first sign to him that he would one day be free.

7. To what did Douglass attribute his good fortune?
He said his good fortune was from God.

8. What did Mrs. Auld teach Douglass to do? What did Mr. Auld say when he found out?
She taught Douglass the alphabet and how to spell some words. Mr. Auld told her to stop. He said that teaching slaves to read made them unmanageable, discontented, and unhappy.

9. What did Douglass think about Mr. Auld's comments? What did Douglass decide to do in light of the comments?
Douglass realized that Mr. Auld was correct. He understood how the white man was able to enslave the black man. Douglass became determined to learn to read.

10. Compare and contrast the treatment of slaves by the slave owners in the city with the slave owners on the plantations.
The slave owners in the city mostly treated their slaves better than the plantation owners did. The slaves in the city had more food, better clothes, and had some privileges.

Assignment 3
Chapters VII-IX

1. How did Mrs. Auld change during the time that Douglass lived with the Auld family? What made her change?
The duties of a slave owner changed her from being a kind, tender-hearted woman to a fierce person with a heart of stone.

2. How did Douglass learn to read?
He made friends with the little white boys. He did his errands quickly and managed a few minutes for lessons with them. With the poor white boys, he traded bread for lessons.

3. How old was Douglass when he read "*The Columbian Orator*"? What effect did this book have on him?
He was twelve when he read the book. The book helped him argue against slavery. The book also made him hate the slave owners.

4. Why did Douglass say that learning to read was a curse instead of a blessing?
Learning to read made him realize how bad his condition was, but reading did not give him a way out of slavery.

5. What word did Douglass hear that was of interest to him? How did he find out the meaning? Why was this word interesting?
He heard the word abolitionists. He found out the meaning by reading newspapers. He realized the word had to do with freeing slaves.

6. Describe how Douglass learned to write.
While working at the shipyard he learned the names of the letters that were used on the timber. He also learned how to copy the letters. To learn how to write more letters, he challenged boys who could write by telling them he could write as well as they could. He would write the letters he knew and then watch them write additional letters. He also copied the italics in Webster's Spelling Book. Once young Thomas Auld was in school, Douglass copied the writing in Auld's copybooks.

7. What event happened about three years after Douglass began living in Baltimore that again reminded him that he detested slavery?
His master, Captain Anthony, died suddenly. Since he did not have a will, all of his property, including the slaves, had to be sent back to his homestead to be valued. Douglass expressed his dislike of the process of being valued and then the slaves dispersed against their will.

8. What regret did Douglass express about the time when he was moved from Master Hugh's home to Master Thomas? Why did he have this regret?
He regretted not at least trying to run away, because it was easier to escape from a city than from the country.

9. Douglass says that Master Thomas was a mean man. Which of Thomas's practices was considered the meanest, even among slaveholders?
Thomas did not give his slaves enough to eat.

10. Where did Master Thomas send Douglass, for how long, and why?
Thomas sent Douglass to live with Edward Covey for a year. Thomas was not able to handle Douglass, and Covey had a reputation for being able to break the slaves.

Assignment 4

Chapter X

1. What happened to Douglass almost every week for the first six months that he lived with Covey?
Covey whipped him.

2. Douglass says that he was "somewhat unmanageable" when he first went to live with Covey. How does Douglass describe himself after he had been with Covey for a few months?
Covey's discipline tamed and broke Douglass.

3. Summarize Douglass's thoughts when he looked at the ships on the Chesapeake Bay.
He thought it was unfair that the ships were free but he was not free. He vowed to run away. He believed that he was not meant to be a slave forever. He sometimes thought that his misery in slavery would give him more happiness when he was free.

4. What did Covey do to Douglass when he (Douglass) became sick while fanning the wheat?
Covey kicked Douglass in the ribs and hit him in the head with a hickory slat.

5. What did Douglass do as a result of Covey's treatment of him? What was the result of Douglass's actions? What did Douglass do?
Douglass walked to Master Thomas's store, a distance of about seven miles, and asked Thomas to remove him from Covey's supervision. Thomas refused the request and sent Douglass back to live with Covey. Douglass went back as he was ordered.

6. What suggestion did another slave named Sandy Jenkins give to Douglass? What did Douglass do?
Sandy told Douglass to carry a piece of a certain root on his right side and he would never again be whipped by a white slave owner. Douglass put a piece of the root in his pocket, even though he did not really believe it would help.

7. Describe the turning point in Douglass's life as a slave that happened when he was with Covey.
The day after Douglass returned to Covey, Douglass resisted as Covey was trying to whip him. Douglass managed to whip Covey, but Covey was not able to hurt Douglass. From this time on, Covey did not again attempt to whip Douglass.

8. According to Douglass, what institution is the "mere covering for the most horrid crimes"? What type of slaveholders are the worst? Why does Douglass think this?
Religion is the covering; religious slaveholders are the worst. The religious slaveholders professed their religion while mistreating the slaves.

9. Describe Douglass's first attempt to run away. Tell who was with him, what the plan was, how far they got in the attempt, and what happened to each of the men after they were caught.
Douglass, Henry Harris, John Harris, Henry Bailey, and Charles Roberts made the attempt. Douglass wrote protections or passes for each of the men, saying that they had liberty to go to Baltimore. They planned to steal a canoe and paddle up the Chesapeake Bay past the Maryland limits. The morning of their scheduled break, they realized they had been discovered. The men were taken to jail in St. Michael's. Mr. Hamilton and Mr. Freeland took all but Douglass out of jail. After about a week, Mr. Auld came for Douglass and sent him back to Baltimore to live with Hugh.

10. What trade did Douglass learn? What was his situation at the end of a year of working at this trade? What was unfair about this situation?
He learned how to calk ships. At the end of a year, he was earning the highest wages of an experienced calker. However, he had to give his wages to Mr. Hugh.

Assignment 5
Chapters XI, Appendix

1. Why didn't Douglass give all of the details of his escape?
He did not want to embarrass anyone who helped; he did not want the slaveholders to know how he escaped.

2. How did Douglass feel about the underground railroad?
He disapproved of the public manner of the system and called it the upperground railroad. He did not think the system was of much help to the slaves because it made the owners more watchful.

3. Master Hugh sometimes gave Douglass six cents of his wages after he had made six dollars, supposedly to encourage him. What effect did this have on Douglass?
It made him restless and discontent because it seemed to him an admission that he deserved all of the money.

4. Why did Douglass want to hire himself out, even though Master Hugh took most of the wages?
Douglass considered hiring himself out a step toward freedom to be allowed to have the responsibilities of a freeman.

5. When did Douglass succeed in escaping? Where did he go? How did Douglass feel when he arrived in the free state?
He left Baltimore on September 3, 1838. He went to New York. He said it was the highest excitement he ever experienced. He wrote that it was like escaping from a den of hungry lions.

6. What motto did Douglass adopt in the free state. Why?
He adopted the motto "Trust no man!" because there were slave hunters all over looking for escaped slaves to capture and return to slavery.

7. Who helped Douglass and what were some of the results of his help?
Mr. David Ruggles helped Douglass by giving him a room in his boarding house and by helping him arrange for Anna, his intended wife, to join them. They were married on September 15, 1838. He also got Douglass a job in New Bedford.

8. Describe how Frederick Bailey took the name of Douglass. Include all of the names he used, including the name his mother gave him.
His mother named him "Frederick Augustus Washington Bailey." When he left Baltimore, he used the name "Stanley." When he got to New York he changed his name to "Frederick Johnson." There were too many people named Johnson, so the man who was helping him, who was also named Johnson, suggested that Bailey take the name of "Douglass" from the book, The Lady of the Lake.

9. What newspaper did Douglass begin to read? How did this newspaper affect his ideas and actions?
Douglass began to read the Liberator. *He liked the ideas about anti-slavery and began attending meetings. On August 11, 1841, while attending a meeting at Nantucket, Douglass reluctantly spoke to the group. From then on, he began speaking out against slavery.*

10. Summarize Douglass's thoughts on the type of Christianity that he calls the slaveholding religion.

The slaveholding religion was totally different from the Christianity of Christ. The slaveholding religion was hypocritical Christianity which served the devil. He considered religion and robbery allies.

Assignment 1
Chapters I-III

1. Which sentence about Frederick Douglass is false?

    A. His birth name was Frederick Augustus Washington Bailey.

    B. He did not know when he was born but estimated that it was around 1818.

    C. He was born in Tuckahoe, near Hillsboro, Maryland.

    D. His parents were both slaves on the same plantation.

2. How old was Frederick Douglass when he wrote his narrative?

    A. He was nineteen.

    B. He was fifty-six.

    C. He was about twenty-seven or twenty-eight.

    D. He was about seventy-one or seventy-two.

3. How long did Frederick Douglass live with his birth mother?

    A. His entire childhood

    B. Until he was two

    C. Less than a year

    D. Until he was five

4. The mulatto children had a slave mother but a white father, who was usually the slave owner. Douglass said that these children _____.

    A. Were usually treated better than the other slaves

    B. Were often killed at birth if the owner's wife requested it

    C. Were often sold off

    D. Were brought up in the master's house along with his other children

5. Douglass thought the presence of the mulatto slaves might do away with the reasoning that since _____, then American slavery was right.

    A. Other countries had slaves

    B. God cursed Ham

    C. White people were more intelligent

    D. African rulers originally sold their own people

6. Who was Douglass's first master?
   A. Captain Aaron Anthony
   B. General George Watkins
   C. Mr. Ebenezer Hastings
   D. Reverend Thomas Miller

7. What was each adult slave's monthly allowance of food?
   A. Four pounds of beef or chicken, a dozen apples, and two bushels of corn
   B. Twelve pounds of pork or beef and three bushels of flour
   C. Thirty eggs, one pound of meat, and five bushels of oats
   D. Eight pounds of pork or fish and one bushel of corn meal

8. Douglass said the slaves sang most when they were ___.
   A. Picking cotton
   B. Happy
   C. Well fed
   D. Unhappy

9. Colonel Lloyd spread _____ on the fence around the garden. If a slave was caught with it on his person, it was proof that the slave had tried to get in the garden, or had been in the garden. The slave was punished.
   A. Blood
   B. Tar
   C. Mud
   D. Paint

10. According to Douglass, what kind of comments did slaves usually make about their owners?
    A. Truthful
    B. Complaining
    C. Nonsensical
    D. Complimentary

Assignment 2
Chapters IV-VI

1. Which three words does Douglass use to describe Mr. Gore?

    A. Intelligent, methodical, and selfish

    B. Irresponsible, sadistic, and grim

    C. Uncooperative, moody, and sneaky

    D. Cruel, artful, and obdurate

2. Mr. Gore shot and killed Demby when Demby refused to come out of the creek where he had taken refuge from a beating. What punishment did he receive?

    A. His guns were taken away for one year.

    B. Gore was not punished.

    C. He was fined one dollar.

    D. He spent a week in jail.

3. What did Mr. Thomas Lanman, Mrs. Hick, and Mr. Beal Bondy have in common?

    A. Each of them owned Frederick Douglass at some point in his life.

    B. They were all atheists.

    C. They were all white slave owners who were kind and good masters.

    D. They were all white slave owners who killed slaves.

4. How did Master Daniel Lloyd treat Frederick Douglass?

    A. He teased him and beat him.

    B. He took Frederick fishing and to church with him.

    C. He shared food with him and protected him.

    D. He always tried to get Douglass in trouble.

5. When he was about seven or eight, Douglass was sent to Baltimore to live with Mr. Hugh Auld and his family. What was his job there?

    A. Tending the family gardens

    B. Taking care of the Aulds' young son, Thomas

    C. Cleaning the kitchen

    D. Running errands for Mrs. Auld

6. Douglass thought his departure from Colonel Lloyd's plantation was _____.
    A. A punishment for his misbehavior
    B. The end of his life
    C. An opportunity to meet new people
    D. The first sign to him that he would one day be free

7. Douglass said his good fortune was _____.
    A. Because of the generosity of Colonel Lloyd
    B. From God
    C. Due to his own hard work
    D. Something that every slave deserved

8. What did Mrs. Auld teach Douglass?
    A. The alphabet and how to spell some words
    B. How to add and subtract
    C. How to read a map
    D. To speak French

9. When Mr. Auld found out Mrs. Auld had been teaching Frederick, he made her stop, saying education made the slaves unhappy and unmanageable. What effect did this have on Frederick Douglass?
    A. He became determined to be the first black man to graduate from college.
    B. He became completely demoralized.
    C. He realized that to be happy he would have to give up education, and he did.
    D. It made him determined to learn to read.

Assignment 3
Chapters VII-IX

1. Mrs. Auld changed from being a kind, tender-hearted woman to a fierce person with a heart of stone. What made her change?

    A. The new preacher she listened to changed her.

    B. The duties of a slave owner changed her.

    C. Mr. Auld began to beat her frequently, which changed her personality.

    D. Her parents died and the grief changed her.

2. How did Douglass learn to read?

    A. He traded bread for lessons with the poor white boys.

    B. He listened to Mrs. Auld reading her Bible aloud.

    C. A worker at the shipyard taught him secretly.

    D. Mr. Auld changed his mind and taught Douglass himself.

3. When Douglas was twelve he read this book. The book helped him argue against slavery. The book also made him hate the slave owners. What is the title of the book?

    A. Dred: A Tale of the Great Dismal Swamp

    B. Unconstitutionality of Slavery

    C. The Columbian Orator

    D. Uncle Tom's Cabin

4. Douglass said that learning made him realize how bad his condition was, but _____.

    A. He would not be happy until he shared his learning with other slaves.

    B. It would also provide him the means to make his life better.

    C. Reading did not give him a way out of slavery.

    D. He was still glad to know more about the world.

5. What word did Douglass hear that was of interest to him?

    A. Tubman

    B. Quaker

    C. Canada

    D. Abolitionists

6.	How did Douglass first begin to learn to write?
	A.	By copying the letters on the timber at the shipyard
	B.	By holding Thomas's hand while he wrote his homework
	C.	By drawing letters in the air while he was walking
	D.	By running his fingers over the letters in the Bible

7.	What happened to Douglass when Captain Anthony died?
	A.	He was sent back to Anthony's homestead to be valued and counted.
	B.	He was given a gift of ten dollars.
	C.	He was given one day off for mourning.
	D.	He was permitted to attend the funeral.

8.	What did Douglass regret when he was moved from Master Hugh's home to Master Thomas's?
	A.	Not saying goodbye to his friends
	B.	Not trying to run away
	C.	Not taking his books with him
	D.	Not thanking Master Hugh

9.	Douglass says that Master Thomas was a mean man. Which of Thomas's practices was considered the meanest, even among slaveholders?
	A.	Thomas did not give his slaves enough to eat.
	B.	Thomas did not let the slaves talk to each other.
	C.	Thomas did not give any clothes to the children.
	D.	Thomas did not let his slaves rest on Sunday.

10.	Why did Master Thomas send Douglass to live with Edward Covey for a year?
	A.	Because Covey had a reputation for being able to successfully breed the slaves
	B.	Because Covey had a reputation for being able to break the slaves
	C.	Because Covey had a reputation for being able to teach the slaves better manners
	D.	Because Covey had a reputation for being able to train slaves as carpenters

Assignment 4
Chapter X

1. What happened to Douglass almost every week for the first six months that he lived with Covey?

    A. He walked back to Master Thomas's house every Saturday.

    B. He held secret reading lessons for other slaves.

    C. Covey whipped him.

    D. He went to church.

2. How does Douglass describe himself after he had been with Covey for a few months?

    A. He says Covey's discipline tamed and broke him.

    B. He says Covey's friendship made him believe there was hope for the slaves.

    C. He describes himself as robust, happy, and content.

    D. He describes himself as gaunt and weak from being deprived of food.

3. Douglass thought it was unfair that the _____ were free but he was not free.

    A. Ships on the Chesapeake Bay

    B. Ants on the ground

    C. Poor white servants

    D. Birds in the air

4. What did Covey do to Douglass when he (Douglass) became sick while fanning the wheat?

    A. Covey kicked Douglass in the ribs and hit him in the head with a hickory slat.

    B. Covey took him to a doctor.

    C. Covey gave him water and made him go back into the fields.

    D. Covey sent him to the main house to rest.

5. Douglass walked to Master Thomas's store, a distance of about seven miles, and asked Thomas to remove him from Covey's supervision. What was Thomas's response?

    A. Thomas agreed and brought Douglass to his home.

    B. Thomas refused the request and sent Douglass back to live with Covey.

    C. Thomas gave him a room behind the store and let him work at the store.

    D. Thomas whipped Douglass for asking.

6. Another slave named Sandy Jenkins told Douglass to carry _____on his right side and he would never again be whipped by a white slave owner.
    A. A copper coin
    B. A rabbit's foot
    C. A piece of a certain root
    D. A dried flower

7. What happened when Douglass beat Covey?
    A. Douglass was immediately sold.
    B. Covey never whipped Douglass again.
    C. Douglass realized his mistake and begged for forgiveness.
    D. Covey got even with Douglass later by beating him more frequently after that.

8. According to Douglass, this is the "mere covering for the most horrid crimes."
    A. Love
    B. Prejudice
    C. Religion
    D. Profit

9. What happened to Douglass when he got caught during his first attempt to get away?
    A. Mr. Auld sent him to Baltimore to live with Hugh.
    B. Hugh sent him to work in Alabama.
    C. He was sentenced to five years in jail.
    D. He was whipped and sent home.

10. What trade did Douglass learn?
    A. Drying tobacco
    B. Repairing wagons
    C. Ship caulking
    D. Horse shoeing

Assignment 5
Chapters XI, Appendix

1. Douglass did not give all of the details of his escape because he did not want to embarrass anyone who helped, and what other reason?
    A. He thought each slave should find his or her own way.
    B. He did not want the slaveholders to know how he escaped.
    C. He was afraid the slave catchers would find him.
    D. He did not remember all of them.

2. How did Douglass feel about the underground railroad?
    A. He didn't believe in it.
    B. He didn't think it was of much help to the slaves because it made the owners more watchful.
    C. He thought it was a great idea and well-done.
    D. He thought it was just a trap to lure slaves into trouble.

3. Master Hugh sometimes gave Douglass six cents of his wages after he had made six dollars, supposedly to encourage him. How did it make him feel?
    A. Rich and happy
    B. Worthless
    C. Eager to work more
    D. Restless and discontented

4. Douglass considered _____ a step toward freedom.
    A. Hiring himself out
    B. Buying a pair of shoes
    C. Getting married
    D. Talking to white men

5. When did Douglass succeed in escaping? Where did he go?
    A. He left Baltimore on September 3, 1838. He went to New York.
    B. He left Baltimore on November 9, 1840. He went to Canada.
    C. He left Baltimore on December 25, 1841. He went to Kansas.
    D. He left Baltimore on July 17, 1837. He went to Philadelphia.

6. What motto did Douglass adopt in the free state?
   A. Trust no man!
   B. To thine own self be true.
   C. Give me liberty or give me death!
   D. Don't tread on me!

7. Which of the following is NOT something Mr. David Ruggles did for Frederick Douglass?
   A. Gave him a room in his boarding house
   B. Helped Douglass get his diploma
   C. Helped arrange for Anna's arrival
   D. Got Douglass a job in New Bedford

8. The man who was helping Frederick suggested that he should take the name of "Douglass" from _____.
   A. A freedom fighter from Scotland
   B. The name of a strong, sturdy tree
   C. His father, who was a famous abolitionist
   D. The book *The Lady of the Lake*

9. What newspaper did Douglass begin to read?
   A. New York Times
   B. Underground Railroad Gazette
   C. Anti-Slavery Journal
   D. Liberator

10. What was the primary characteristic of "slaveholding religion"?
    A. Greed
    B. Hypocrisy
    C. Truthfulness
    D. Peace

ANSWER KEY: STUDY QUESTIONS *Narrative of the Life of Frederick Douglass*

	1	2	3	4	5
1	D	D	B	C	B
2	C	B	A	A	B
3	C	D	C	A	D
4	C	C	C	A	A
5	B	B	D	B	A
6	A	D	A	C	A
7	D	B	A	B	B
8	D	A	B	C	D
9	B	D	A	A	D
10	D		B	C	B

VOCABULARY WORKSHEETS

VOCABULARY ASSIGNMENT 1 *Narrative of the Life of Frederick Douglass*

Part I: Using Prior Knowledge and Contextual Clues
    Below are the sentences in which the vocabulary words appear in the text. Read the sentence. Use any clues you can find in the sentence combined with your prior knowledge, and write what you think the underlined words mean on the lines provided.

1. I have no accurate knowledge of my age, never having seen any <u>authentic</u> record containing it.

   _____

2. He deemed all such inquiries on the part of a slave improper and <u>impertinent,</u> and evidence of a restless spirit.

   _____

3. . . . whilst the fact remains, in all its glaring <u>odiousness,</u> that slaveholders have ordained . . . .

   _____

4. Why master was so careful of her, may be safely left to <u>conjecture.</u>

   _____

5. I did not, when a slave, understand the deep meaning of those rude and apparently <u>incoherent</u> songs.

   _____

6. . . . and if he is not thus impressed, it will only be because "there is no flesh in his <u>obdurate</u> heart."

   _____

7. The singing of a man cast away upon a <u>desolate</u> island might be as appropriately considered as evidence of contentment and happiness . . . .

   _____

8. They seemed to realize the impossibility of touching tar without being <u>defiled.</u>

   _____

9. . . . and thus, without a moment's warning, he was snatched away, and forever <u>sundered,</u> from his family and friends, by a hand more unrelenting than death.

   _____

10. . . . the frequency of this has had the effect to establish among the slaves the <u>maxim,</u> that a still tongue makes a wise head.

   _____

Narrative of the Life of Frederick Douglass Vocabulary Worksheet Assignment 1 Continued

Part II: Determining the Meaning -- Match the vocabulary words to their dictionary definitions.

____ 1.	AUTHENTIC	A.	Separated
____ 2.	IMPERTINENT	B.	Having one's good name ruined
____ 3.	ODIOUSNESS	C.	Stubborn
____ 4.	CONJECTURE	D.	Deserted; uninhabited
____ 5.	INCOHERENT	E.	Being full of hatred
____ 6.	OBDURATE	F.	Rambling; confused; disjointed
____ 7.	DESOLATE	G.	Guessing
____ 8.	DEFILED	H.	Saying; a truth
____ 9.	SUNDERED	I.	Rude; disrespectful
____ 10.	MAXIM	J.	Genuine; real

VOCABULARY ASSIGNMENT 2 *Narrative of the Life of Frederick Douglass*

Part I: Using Prior Knowledge and Contextual Clues

    Below are the sentences in which the vocabulary words appear in the text. Read the sentence. Use any clues you can find in the sentence combined with your prior knowledge, and write what you think the underlined words mean on the lines provided.

1. No matter how innocent a slave might be--it <u>availed</u> him nothing, when accused by Mr. Gore of any misdemeanor.

    _____

2. To be accused was to be convicted, and to be convicted was to be punished; the one always following the other with <u>immutable</u> certainty.

    _____

3. His savage barbarity was equaled only by the <u>consummate</u> coolness with which he committed the grossest and most savage deeds upon the slaves under his charge.

    _____

4. Colonel Lloyd's slaves were in the habit of spending a part of their nights and Sundays in fishing for oysters, and in this way made up the <u>deficiency</u> of their scanty allowance.

    _____

5. Colonel Lloyd's slaves were in the habit of spending a part of their nights and Sundays in fishing for oysters, and in this way made up the deficiency of their <u>scanty</u> allowance.

    _____

6. I wish I could describe the <u>rapture</u> that flashed through my soul as I beheld it.

    _____

7. I have ever regarded it as the first plain <u>manifestation</u> of that kind providence which has ever since attended me, and marked my life with so many favors.

    _____

8. I have ever regarded it as the first plain manifestation of that kind <u>providence</u> which has ever since attended me, and marked my life with so many favors.

    _____

9. I prefer to be true to myself, even at the hazard of incurring the ridicule of others, rather than to be false, and incur my own <u>abhorrence</u>.

    _____

10. I now understood what had been to me a most <u>perplexing</u> difficulty--to wit, the white man's power to enslave the black man.

    _____

Part II: Determining the Meaning -- Match the vocabulary words to their dictionary definitions.

_____ 1.	AVAILED	A.	Care or guardianship exercised by a deity
_____ 2.	IMMUTABLE	B.	Made useful; helped
_____ 3.	CONSUMMATE	C.	Less than is needed
_____ 4.	DEFICIENCY	D.	Not changeable
_____ 5.	SCANTY	E.	Complete
_____ 6.	RAPTURE	F.	Expression; revelation; display
_____ 7.	MANIFESTATION	G.	Delight; joy
_____ 8.	PROVIDENCE	H.	Intense disapproval or dislike
_____ 9.	ABHORRENCE	I.	Lack; shortage
_____ 10.	PERPLEXING	J.	Puzzling; confusing

Part I: Using Prior Knowledge and Contextual Clues

    Below are the sentences in which the vocabulary words appear in the text. Read the sentence. Use any clues you can find in the sentence combined with your prior knowledge, and write what you think the underlined words mean on the lines provided.

1. She at first lacked the <u>depravity</u> indispensable to shutting me up in mental darkness.

   _____

2. The slave was made to say some very smart as well as impressive things in reply to his master--things which had the desired though unexpected effect; for the conversation resulted in the voluntary <u>emancipation</u> of the slave on the part of the master.

   _____

3. What I got from Sheridan was a bold <u>denunciation</u> of slavery, and a powerful vindication of human rights.

   _____

4. What I got from Sheridan was a bold denunciation of slavery, and a powerful <u>vindication</u> of human rights.

   _____

5. Here again my feelings rose up in <u>detestation</u> of slavery.

   _____

6. He was known to us all as being a most cruel wretch,--a common drunkard, who had, by his reckless mismanagement and <u>profligate</u> dissipation, already wasted a large portion of his father's property.

   _____

7. He could not come among us without betraying his sympathy for us, and, stupid as we were, we had the <u>sagacity</u> to see it.

   _____

8. Bad as all slaveholders are, we seldom meet one <u>destitute</u> of every element of character commanding respect.

   _____

9. My city life, he said, had had a very <u>pernicious</u> effect upon me.

   _____

Part II: Determining the Meaning -- Match the vocabulary words to their dictionary definitions.

____ 1.	DEPRAVITY	A.	Wasteful; extremely extravagant
____ 2.	EMANCIPATION	B.	Condemnation; criticism
____ 3.	DENUNCIATION	C.	Totally lacking
____ 4.	VINDICATION	D.	Setting free
____ 5.	DETESTATION	E.	Support; justification
____ 6.	PROFLIGATE	F.	Wisdom
____ 7.	SAGACITY	G.	Evil; wickedness
____ 8.	DESTITUTE	H.	Hatred; loathing
____ 9.	PERNICIOUS	I.	Destructive; harmful

VOCABULARY ASSIGNMENT 4 *Narrative of the Life of Frederick Douglass*

Part I: Using Prior Knowledge and Contextual Clues
    Below are the sentences in which the vocabulary words appear in the text. Read the sentence. Use any clues you can find in the sentence combined with your prior knowledge, and write what you think the underlined words mean on the lines provided.

1. When he saw Hughes bending over with pain, his courage <u>quailed</u>.

    _____

2. They are professedly a custom established by the <u>benevolence</u> of the slaveholders; but I undertake to say, it is the result of selfishness, and one of the grossest frauds committed upon the down-trodden slave.

    _____

3. Does he ever venture to vindicate his conduct, when <u>censured</u> for it?

    _____

4. Then he is guilty of <u>impudence</u>,--one of the greatest crimes of which a slave can be guilty.

    _____

5. I had at one time over forty scholars, and those of the right sort, <u>ardently</u> desiring to learn.

    _____

6. I therefore, though with great prudence, commenced early to ascertain their views and feelings in regard to their condition, and to <u>imbue</u> their minds with thoughts of freedom.

    _____

7. This in itself was sometimes enough to stagger us; but when we permitted ourselves to survey the road, we were frequently <u>appalled</u>.

    _____

8. We went, as usual, to our several fields of labor, but with bosoms highly <u>agitated</u> with thoughts of our truly hazardous undertaking.

    _____

9. Such a set of beings I never saw before. I felt myself surrounded by so many fiends from <u>perdition</u>. A band of pirates never looked more like their father, the devil.

    _____

10. It is necessary to darken his moral and mental vision, and, as far as possible, to <u>annihilate</u> the power of reason.

    _____

Part II: Determining the Meaning -- Match the vocabulary words to their dictionary definitions.

____ 1.	QUAILED	A.	Drew back in fear
____ 2.	BENEVOLENCE	B.	Kindness; compassion; good will
____ 3.	CENSURED	C.	State of everlasting punishment; hell
____ 4.	IMPUDENCE	D.	Anxious; nervous
____ 5.	ARDENTLY	E.	Severely criticized
____ 6.	IMBUE	F.	Shocked; horrified
____ 7.	APPALLED	G.	Fill
____ 8.	AGITATED	H.	Destroy
____ 9.	PERDITION	I.	Enthusiastically
____ 10.	ANNIHILATE	J.	Rude behavior

VOCABULARY ASSIGNMENT 5 *Narrative of the Life of Frederick Douglass*

Part I: Using Prior Knowledge and Contextual Clues

    Below are the sentences in which the vocabulary words appear in the text. Read the sentence. Use any clues you can find in the sentence combined with your prior knowledge, and write what you think the underlined words mean on the lines provided.

1. Secondly, such a statement would most undoubtedly induce greater <u>vigilance</u> on the part of slaveholders than has existed heretofore among them . . . .

_____

2. I would allow myself to suffer under the greatest <u>imputations</u> which evil-minded men might suggest, rather than exculpate myself, and thereby run the hazard of closing the slightest avenue by which a brother slave might clear himself of the chains an

_____

3. I would allow myself to suffer under the greatest imputations which evil-minded men might suggest, rather than <u>exculpate</u> myself, and thereby run the hazard of closing the slightest avenue by which a brother slave might clear himself of the chains and fetters of slavery.

_____

4. I would leave him to imagine himself surrounded by <u>myriads</u> of invisible tormentors, ever ready to snatch from his infernal grasp his trembling prey.

_____

5. Let him be left to feel his way in the dark; let darkness <u>commensurate</u> with his crime hover over him. . . .

_____

6. He <u>exhorted</u> me to content myself, and be obedient.

_____

7. I spent the whole week without the performance of a single stoke of work. I did this in <u>retaliation</u>.

_____

8. I had somehow <u>imbibed</u> the opinion that, in the absence of slaves, there could be no wealth, and very little refinement.

_____

9. My soul was set all on fire. Its sympathy for my brethren in bonds--its <u>scathing</u> denunciation of slaveholders--and its powerful attacks upon the upholders of the institution--sent a thrill of joy through my soul, such as I had never felt before.

_____

10. They would be shocked at the proposition of fellowshipping a sheep-stealer; and at the same time they hug to their communion a man-stealer, and brand me with being an <u>infidel</u>, if I find fault with them for it.

_____

Part II: Determining the Meaning -- Match the vocabulary words to their dictionary definitions.

____ 1.	VIGILANCE	A. Care; watchfulness
____ 2.	IMPUTATIONS	B. Accusations
____ 3.	EXCULPATE	C. Urged; insisted
____ 4.	MYRIADS	D. Equal
____ 5.	COMMENSURATE	E. Scornful; mocking
____ 6.	EXHORTED	F. Took into the mind; absorbed
____ 7.	RETALIATION	G. To free from blame
____ 8.	IMBIBED	H. A person without belief in the religion of the writer
____ 9.	SCATHING	I. Huge numbers
____ 10.	INFIDEL	J. Revenge; getting even

VOCABULARY ANSWER KEY - *Narrative of the Life of Frederick Douglass*

	1	2	3	4	5
1	J	B	G	A	A
2	I	D	D	B	B
3	E	E	B	E	G
4	G	I	E	J	I
5	F	C	H	I	D
6	C	G	A	G	C
7	D	F	F	F	J
8	B	A	C	D	F
9	A	H	I	C	E
10	H	J		H	H

DAILY LESSONS

LESSON ONE

Objectives

1. To introduce the unit on *Narrative of the Life of Frederick Douglass, an American Slave*
2. To distribute books, study guides and other related materials
3. To complete a KWL related to Frederick Douglass
4. To give students background information about *Narrative of the Life of Frederick Douglass, an American Slave* and slavery

Activity 1

Distribute books, study guides, and reading assignments. Explain in detail how students are to use these materials.

Study Guides Students should preview the study guide questions before each reading assignment to get a feeling for what events and ideas are important in that section. After reading the section, students will (as a class or individually) answer the question to review the important events and ideas from that section of the book. Students should keep the study guides as study materials for the unit test.

Reading Assignment Sheet You (the teachers) need to fill in the Reading Assignment Sheet to let students know when their reading has to be completed. You can either write the assignment sheet on a side blackboard or bulletin board and leave it there for students to see each day, or you can duplicate copies for each student to have. In either case, you should advise students to become very familiar with the reading assignments so they know what is expected of them.

Unit Outline You may find it helpful to distribute copies of the Unit Outline to your students so they can keep track of upcoming lessons and assignments. You may also want to post a copy of the Unit Outline on a bulletin board and cross off each lesson as you complete it.

Extra Activities Center The Extra Activities Packet portion of this unit contains suggestions for a library of related books and articles in your classroom as well as crossword and word search puzzles. Make an extra activities center in your classroom where you will keep these materials for students to use. Bring the books and articles in from the library and keep several copies of the puzzles on hand. Explain to students that these materials are available for students to use when they finish reading assignments or other class work early.

Books Each school has its own rules and regulations regarding student use of school books. Advise students of the procedures that are normal for your school.

Notebook or Unit Folder You may want the students to keep all of their worksheets, notes, and other papers for the unit together in a binder or notebook. During the first class meeting, tell them how you want them to arrange the folder. Make divider pages for vocabulary worksheets, Prereading study guide questions, review activities, notes, and tests. You may want to give a grade for accuracy in keeping the folder.

Activity 2

Ask students to tell you what they know about slavery the United States in the early to mid 1800s, and anything they know about Frederick Douglass in particular. Do a group KWL with students (included in this Lit Plan.) Write any information the students know in the K column (What I Know). Ask students what they want to find out and write those questions in the W column (What I Want to Find Out.) Keep the KWL sheet and refer back to it as students read the book. After reading the book, work with the group to complete the L column (What I Learned.)

Activity 3
Conduct one of the following activities or a similar activity with students. Make up a fill-in-the-blank worksheet to go along with the activity. The purposes of the worksheet are to keep students' attention on the topic, to provide students with a guide to the points you want them to remember, and to give students a good study guide for the background information. A worksheet is not included in this Lit Plan because of the variety of options for the lesson.

--Show the PBS documentary titled Africans in America: Part Four: 1831-1865. This part of the series features Frederick Douglass as one of the topics. More information can be found at the Web site: http://www.pbs.org/wgbh/aia/part4/4p1539.html.

--Show students some of Frederick Douglass's papers, available from the Library of Congress, and accessible on the Library's Web site: http://memory.loc.gov/ammem/doughtml/doughome.html

--Conduct a virtual field trip to the Frederick Douglass National Historic Site. The Web site has biographical information about Douglass as well as a virtual tour of his home: http://www.nps.gov/archive/frdo/freddoug.html.

--Conduct a virtual field trip to the National Park Service American Visionaries: Frederick Douglass Web site. The site shows some of Douglass's memorabilia and papers, and also gives biographical information: http://www.cr.nps.gov/museum/exhibits/douglass.

Discuss the activity and the answers to the worksheet in the remaining time.

KWL

Narrative of the Life of Frederick Douglass, an American Slave

Directions: Before reading, think about what you already know about Frederick Douglass and/or slavery in the United States in the early to mid 1800s. Write the information in the **K** column. Think about what you would like to find out from reading the book. Write your questions in the **W** column. After you have read the book, use the **L** column to write the answers to your questions from the W column, and anything else you remember from the book.

K What I Know	W What I Want to Find Out	L What I Learned

LESSON TWO

<u>Objectives</u>

1. To learn about topics related to *The Narrative of the Life of Frederick Douglass*
2. To encourage students to expand beyond the text
3. To practice researching skills
4. To evaluate students' non-fiction reading experience

<u>Activity</u>

Distribute copies of the Non-fiction Assignment Sheet and go over it in detail with the students. Explain to students that they each are to read at least one non-fiction piece at some time during the unit. This could be a book, a magazine article, or information from an encyclopedia or the Internet.

Students will fill out a Non-fiction Assignment Sheet after completing the reading to help you (the teacher) evaluate their reading experiences and to help the students think about and evaluate their own reading.

Encourage students to read about topics that are related to the theme of the novel. There is a list of suggested related topics in the Unit Resource Materials section.

Give students the remainder of the class period to begin working on their non-fiction assignments. Encourage them to brainstorm a list of ideas before finalizing their topics.

NON-FICTION ASSIGNMENT SHEET
Narrative of the Life of Frederick Douglass, an American Slave

(To be completed after reading the required non-fiction article.)

Name _____ Date _____ Class _____

Title of Non-fiction Read _____

Written by _____ Publication Date _____

Web Site Address (if applicable) _____

I. Factual Summary: Write a summary of the piece you read.

II. Vocabulary:
    1. Which vocabulary words were difficult?

    2. What did you do to help yourself understand the words?

III. Interpretation: What was the main point the author wanted you to get from reading his/her work?

IV. Criticism:
    1. Which points of the piece did you agree with or find easy to believe? Why?

    2. With which points of the piece did you disagree or find difficult to believe? Why?

V. Personal Response:
    1. What did you think about this piece?

    2. How does this piece help you understand the autobiography *Narrative of the Life of Frederick Douglass, an American Slave*?

LESSON THREE

Objectives
1. To preview the study questions and do the vocabulary work for Chapters I-III
2. To understand the characteristics of an autobiography
3. To read Chapters I-III

Activity 1

Show students how to preview the study questions using the questions for Chapters I-III, and do the vocabulary work for Chapters I-III orally together in class.

Encourage students to take notes when they read. If students own their books, encourage them to use highlighters or colored pens to mark important passages and the answers to the study guide questions.

Activity 2

Explain to students that *Narrative of the Life of Frederick Douglass, an American Slave* is an autobiography. An autobiography is an account of a person's life written by that person. An autobiography usually covers a span of at least several years. It will include names and descriptions of people, dates and details of events, and descriptions of places. The author may choose to include information about his or her feelings and thoughts as well. Some authors write only from memory, but others may have kept journals for a length of time and refer to them while writing. Information in the autobiography should be factually correct.

Invite students to discuss any familiar autobiographies. Ask them to summarize the information they read and to tell what they liked and/or did not like about the autobiography.

Activity 3

Read Chapter 1 aloud to students to set the mood for the autobiography. Then have students read chapters II-III orally. Either call on students or ask for volunteers, whichever works best with your class. Be sure to give students who need practice reading orally the opportunity to do so, even if it slows down the reading schedule a little. There is an Oral Reading Evaluation Form included in this packet for your convenience.

ORAL READING EVALUATION
Narrative of the Life of Frederick Douglass, an American Slave

Name _____ Class _____ Date _____

SKILL	EXCELLENT	GOOD	AVERAGE	FAIR	POOR
FLUENCY	5	4	3	2	1
CLARITY	5	4	3	2	1
AUDIBILITY	5	4	3	2	1
PRONUNCIATION	5	4	3	2	1
_____	5	4	3	2	1
_____	5	4	3	2	1
_____	5	4	3	2	1

Total Grade:

Comments:

LESSON FOUR

Objectives

1. To review the main events and ideas from Chapters I-III
2. To experience writing an autobiography
3. To connect with Frederick Douglass at least on the experience of writing an autobiography
4. To learn how thinking and writing about past events can affect us
5. To evaluate students' writing skills

Activity 1

Give students a few minutes to formulate answers for the study guide questions for Chapters I-III, then discuss the answers to the questions in detail. Write the answers on the board or overhead transparency so students can have the correct answers for study purposes.

NOTE: It is a good practice in public speaking and leadership skills for individual students to take charge of leading the discussions of the study questions. Perhaps a different student could go to the front of the class and lead the discussion each day that the study questions are discussed in this unit. Of course, you should guide the discussion when appropriate and try to fill in any gaps students may leave. The study questions could really be handled in a number of different ways, including in small groups with group reports following. Occasionally you may want to use the multiple choice questions as quizzes to check students' reading comprehension. As a short review now and then, students could pair up for the first (or last, if you have time left at the end of a class period) few minutes of class to quiz each other from the study questions. Mix up methods of reviewing the materials and checking comprehension throughout the unit so students don't get bored just answering the questions the same way each day. Variety in methods will also help address the different learning styles of your students. From now on in this unit, the directions will simply say, "Discuss the answers to the study questions in detail as previously directed." You will choose the method of preparation and discussion each day based on what best suits you and your class.

Activity 2

Distribute Writing Assignment #1 and discuss the directions in detail. Allow students the remainder of the class period to work on this assignment. Give students an additional two or three class periods to complete the assignment if necessary.

Explain to students that during Lesson Seven you will be holding individual writing conferences about this writing assignment.

WRITING ASSIGNMENT #1 *Narrative of the Life of Frederick Douglass*

PROMPT

Narrative of the Life of Frederick Douglass, an American Slave is an autobiography. The author and narrator, Frederick Douglass, writes about the important people and details in his life. He includes information about his thoughts and feelings as well. Your writing assignment is to write an autobiographical sketch. Douglass's autobiography covered many years of his life. However, your sketch will only cover a short period of time, perhaps a year or two.

PREWRITING

Make a timeline that starts with your birth and continues through the present time. Record as many important events on the timeline as you can. Write down the dates if you remember them. Choose a period of time, such as a year, to write about. Circle that period on your timeline. Then make a separate list of all the events on the timeline for that year. Include details about the people and places involved in each event. Also include your thoughts and feelings.

DRAFTING

Write your first draft. Refer to the timeline and list you developed as you write. Completely describe one event before you move on to the next one. Check to make sure you are including your thoughts and feelings. Use as many descriptive words and images as you can. You may want to use a thesaurus to help you get a variety of words and their exact meanings.

PEER EDITING

When you finish the rough draft of your autobiographical sketch, ask another student to read it. After reading your rough draft, the student should tell you what he/she liked best about your work, which parts were difficult to understand, and ways in which your work could be improved. Your reader should also be able to summarize the main events in your autobiographical sketch. Reread your text considering your critic's comments, and make the revisions you think are necessary.

PROOFREADING/EDITING/FINAL DRAFT

Do a final proofreading of your autobiography, double checking your grammar, spelling, organization, and the clarity of your ideas. Turn the piece into your teacher for grading. Follow your teacher's guidelines for completing the final draft of your piece.

WRITING EVALUATION FORM
Narrative of the Life of Frederick Douglass, an American Slave

Name _____ Date _____ Class _____

Writing Assignment # _____

Circle One for Each Item:

Composition	Excellent	Good	Fair	Poor
Style	Excellent	Good	Fair	Poor
Grammar	Excellent	Good	Fair	Poor
Spelling	Excellent	Good	Fair	Poor
Punctuation	Excellent	Good	Fair	Poor
Legibility	Excellent	Good	Fair	Poor

Strengths:

Weaknesses:

Comments/Suggestions:

LESSON FIVE

Objectives
1. To preview the study questions and do the vocabulary worksheet for Chapters IV-VI
2. To read Chapters IV-VI
3. To practice oral reading
4. To evaluate students' oral reading

Activity 1

Give students about ten or fifteen minutes to preview the study guide questions and complete the vocabulary worksheet for Chapters IV-VI.

After students have ample time to complete the vocabulary work, take a few minutes to discuss the correct answers.

Activity 2

Tell students their oral reading ability will be evaluated today as they read portions from Chapter IV. Show them copies of the Oral Reading Evaluation form and discuss it. Model correct intonation and expression by reading the first few paragraphs of Chapter IV aloud.

Activity 3

Call on individual students to read a few paragraphs from Chapters IV-VI orally. Encourage the other students to follow along in their books. If you have a student who is unwilling or unable to read aloud in front of the group, make arrangements to do his or her evaluation privately at another time. Mark the oral reading evaluation forms as the students read. If all students have read orally before the chapters have been completed, assign the remainder of the text as individual silent reading.

All students should complete reading Chapters IV-VI prior to the next class meeting.

LESSON SIX

Objectives
1. To review the main events and ideas from Chapters IV-VI
2. To complete any unfinished assignments so far
3. To study for a quiz

Activity 1
Discuss the answers to the study questions for Chapters IV-VI as previously directed in Lesson Four.

Activity 2
Tell students they will have a quiz on Chapters I-VI during the next class period. Ask students if they have any questions about the material covered so far. Give students time to go through their study guides and notes to see if they are missing any information. Provide assistance as necessary.

Activity 3
Give students the remainder of this class period to study for the quiz, clean up their notes, complete any unanswered study questions or vocabulary worksheets in their notebooks, finish the first writing assignment, or study. Students whose notebooks are in good order and who have completed the first writing assignment may work together in pairs or small groups to study.

LESSON SEVEN

Objectives
1. To demonstrate understanding of the main events and ideas in Chapters I-VI
2. To participate in an individual writing conference
3. To rewrite Writing Assignment #1 based on the results of the writing conference
4. To preview the study questions and do the vocabulary workseet for Chapters VII-IX
5. To read Chapters VII-IX

Activity 1
Quiz-Distribute quizzes and give students ample time to complete them. Correct and grade the papers as a class. You may want to have students exchange papers or allow them to correct their own work. Collect the quizzes for recording the grades or reviewing student progress.

Activity 2
Ask students what difficulties they faced when writing their mini-autobiographies in Writing Assignment #1. Allow time for some class discussion about the emotional effects of thinking through the past. How did students feel as they remembered certain events or people? Do they feel any differently now about some things than they did when the events took place? How did writing about the events affect students as they wrote? How difficult or easy was it to put down on paper the thoughts and feelings related to the events they related?

Ask students to take a minute to think about how Frederick Douglass must have felt re-living certain events as he wrote his narrative. Have students share their thoughts about this orally in a short discussion.

Transition: Tell students that while they work on the next assignment (Activity 3), you will be holding individual writing conferences to discuss individual students' particular strengths and difficulties relating to the assignment.

Activity 3
Give students the remainder of this class period to preview the study questions, do the vocabulary worksheet, and complete the reading for Chapters VII-IX. Tell students whether they will be working independently or in small groups. Remind students this assignment must be completed prior to the next class period.

Activity 4
While students are working on Activity 2, call students individually to your desk or some other private area of the classroom. Discuss their papers from Writing Assignment #1. Use the completed Writing Evaluation form as a basis for your critique.

LESSON EIGHT

<u>Objectives</u>

1. To review the main events and ideas from Chapters VII-IX
2. To discuss the element of tone in Frederick Douglass's writing
3. To preview the study questions and do the vocabulary work for Chapter X
4. To read Chapter X

<u>Activity 1</u>

Review the study questions and vocabulary work for Chapters VII-IX as previously directed in Lesson Four.

<u>Activity 2</u>

Explain to students that tone is the author's way of speaking to the reader. Tone expresses the author's feeling or attitude toward the characters, events, and information in a piece of writing. The author carefully suggests words that help the reader identify the tone. Discuss with students the tone Douglass uses when talking about different people, for example, Covey or Master Hugh. Model reading passages from the book in the tone of voice that Douglass might use if he were talking about the different people or events. Then have students choose a passage and read it aloud. Discuss as a class if the reader used the appropriate tone.

<u>Activity 3</u>

Tell students that prior to the class meeting after next (insert the day of the week) they must have completed the prereading and reading work for Chapter X. They may use the remainder of this class period to review the study questions, do the vocabulary worksheet, and begin the reading for Chapter X.

LESSON NINE

Objectives

1. To watch a video presentation about Frederick Douglass
2. To further educate students about the life and times of Frederick Douglass

Activity

Use this class time to show students the Biography DVD about Frederick Douglass. It should be available to check out from some libraries or movie rental stores, or you can purchase it on line at www.tpet.com, amazon.com, or many other retailers. Running time is 50 minutes.

As students watch the movie, have them fill out the worksheet that follows. This will help ensure they focus on the movie (rather than sleeping, texting, or something else) and will serve as a study sheet.

STUDY GUIDE
BIOGRAPHY'S PRESENTATION
FREDERICK DOUGLASS

1. John Marzalek, Professor of History at Mississippi University, called Frederick Douglass the _____ of the nation during the Civil War.

2. Thomas Battle, of Howard University, called Frederick Douglass a _____ of strength.

3. Frederick Douglass was born on the Eastern Shore of _____, near Tuckahoe Creek in 1818.

4. Frederick Douglass's father was probably Aaron Anthony, his _____.

5. According to Frederick Douglass, the songs of a slave represent the _____ of his heart.

6. Frederick Douglass learned to read while at the plantation of _____.

7. At age 15, Douglass was moved across the Chesapeake Bay to _____.

8. Frederick Douglass learned the trade of _____ in Baltimore, Maryland.

9. The first book Frederick Douglass bought and read was _____ _____, a collection of famous speeches.

10. The _____ _____ was a series of places at strategic distances from the south to the north where runaway slaves were helped and hidden.

11. _____ took a personal role in helping slaves escape to freedom via the Underground Railroad.

12. In 1831 Anna and Frederick devised a plan to help Frederick escape to the north, to _____ _____. Anna met him there, they were married, and they went on to _____, Massachusetts.

13. William Lloyd Garrison was an _____, a person who wanted slavery to end immediately.

14. Frederick Douglass said that _____ [a newspaper published by William Lloyd Garrison] became his meat and his drink.

15. In 1841 a grand anti-slavery convention was held in _____.

16. Frederick Douglass's first public speech was given in _____ in 1841.

17. By 1843, Douglass had started working on the _____ Project with Garrison and had become a voice for the Anti-Slavery Society.

18. In _____ Douglass published his first autobiography, *Narrative of the Life of Frederick Douglass*.

19. Frederick Douglass went to _____ to protect himself from slave catchers after publishing his autobiography.

20. While he was away, _____ purchased Frederick Douglass from his master, and that is how he acquired his freedom.

21. Upon his return to America in 1847, Frederick Douglass moved to _____, NY and began to publish a newspaper called _____.

22. Frederick and Anna had ___ children.

23. John Brown planned to lead a revolution of slaves, starting in _____, but Frederick Douglass chose not to participate.

24. John Brown and his men were hanged for _____.

25. In 1860, _____ ran for President of a divided nation.

26. On April 12, 1861, Confederate troops attacked _____ _____ in South Carolina.

27. Frederick Douglass saw the purpose of the _____ _____ to be the abolition of slavery.

28. On September 22, 1962, President Lincoln announced the _____ _____, freeing all slaves.

29. The 54th Massachusetts was an all _____ unit with white officers.

30. Frederick Douglass spent his final years at _____ _____, his home in Washington, DC.

31. Frederick Douglass was appointed as _____ of the District of Columbia.

32. Frederick Douglass insisted to his dying day that what the _____ _____ had been about was not just a fight between men of valor, but a struggle to establish a nation that could live up to its creed.

33. In 1882, _____ died.

34. Frederick Douglass was also committed to equal rights for _____.

35. Seventeen months after Anna's death, Frederick married _____, a white woman.

36. President Benjamin Harrison recognized Frederick Douglass, making him Minister to _____.

37. Frederick Douglass was born a _____ but died a statesman.

38. Frederick Douglass died of _____ on February 21, 1895 at the age of seventy-eight, at Cedar Hill.

ANSWER KEY: STUDY GUIDE
BIOGRAPHY'S PRESENTATION
FREDERICK DOUGLASS

1. John Marzalek, Professor of History at Mississippi University, called Frederick Douglass the **CONSCIENCE** of the nation during the Civil War.

2. Thomas Battle, of Howard University, called Frederick Douglass a **PILAR or TOWER** of strength.

3. Frederick Douglass was born on the Eastern Shore of **MARYLAND**, near Tuckahoe Creek in 1818.

4. Frederick Douglass's father was probably Aaron Anthony, his **MASTER**.

5. According to Frederick Douglass, the songs of a slave represent the **SORROWS** of his heart.

6. Frederick Douglass learned to read while at the plantation of **HUGH AULD**.

7. At age 15, Douglass was moved across the Chesapeake Bay to **BALTIMORE**.

8. Frederick Douglass learned the trade of **SHIP'S CAULKER** in Baltimore, Maryland.

9. The first book Frederick Douglass bought and read was **THE COLUMBIAN ORATOR**, a collection of famous speeches.

10. The **UNDERGROUND RAILROAD** was a series of places at strategic distances from the south to the north where runaway slaves were helped and hidden.

11. **HARRIET TUBMAN** took a personal role in helping slaves escape to freedom via the Underground Railroad.

12. In 1831 Anna and Frederick devised a plan to help Frederick escape to the north, to **NEW YORK**. Anna met him there, they were married, and they went on to **NEW BEDFORD**, Massachusetts.

13. William Lloyd Garrison was an **IMMEDIATIST**, a person who wanted slavery to end immediately.

14. Frederick Douglass said that **THE LIBERATOR** [a newspaper published by William Lloyd Garrison] became his meat and his drink.

15. In 1841 a grand anti-slavery convention was held in **NANTUCKET**.

16. Frederick Douglass's first public speech was given in **NANTUCKET** in 1841.

17. By 1843, Douglass had started working on the **HUNDRED CONVENTIONS** Project with Garrison and had become a voice for the Anti-Slavery Society.

18. In**1845** Douglass published his first autobiography, *Narrative of the Life of Frederick Douglass*.

19. Frederick Douglass went to **ENGLAND** to protect himself from slave catchers after publishing his autobiography.

20. While he was away, **SOME OF HIS FRIENDS** purchased Frederick Douglass from his master, and that is how he acquired his freedom.

21. Upon his return to America in 1847, Frederick Douglass moved to **ROCHESTER**, NY and began to publish a newspaper called **THE NORTH STAR**.

22. Frederick and Anna had **FIVE** children.

23. John Brown planned to lead a revolution of slaves, starting in **HARPER'S FERRY**, but Frederick Douglass chose not to participate.

24. John Brown and his men were hanged for **TREASON**.

25. In 1860, **LINCOLN** ran for President of a divided nation.

26. On April 12, 1861, Confederate troops attacked **FORT SUMTER** in South Carolina.

27. Frederick Douglass saw the purpose of the **CIVIL WAR** to be the abolition of slavery.

28. On September 22, 1962, President Lincoln announced the **EMANCIPATION PROCLAMATION**, freeing all slaves.

29. The 54th Massachusetts was an all **NEGRO** unit with white officers.

30. Frederick Douglass spent his final years at **CEDAR HILL**, his home in Washington, DC.

31. Frederick Douglass was appointed as **MINISTER** of the District of Columbia.

32. Frederick Douglass insisted to his dying day that what the **CIVIL WAR** had been about was not just a fight between men of valor, but a struggle to establish a nation that could live up to its creed.

33. In 1882, **ANNA** died.

34. Frederick Douglass was also committed to equal rights for **WOMEN**.

35. Seventeen months after Anna's death, Frederick married **HELEN PITTS**, a white woman.

36. President Benjamin Harrison recognized Frederick Douglass, making him Minister to **HATI.**

37. Frederick Douglass was born a **SLAVE** but died a statesman.

38. Frederick Douglass died of **A STROKE** on February 21, 1895 at the age of seventy-eight, at Cedar Hill.

LESSON TEN

Objectives
1. To review the study sheet from the Frederick Douglass Biography movie
2. To review the main events and ideas and vocabulary from Chapter X
3. To learn more about cause and effect

Activity 1
If you watched the Biography movie about Frederick Douglass in your last class meeting, take a few minutes to review the study sheet that accompanied that activity.

Activity 2
Review the study questions and vocabulary work for Chapter X as previously directed in Lesson Four.

Activity 3
Explain to students that a cause is an event, an action, or a behavior that makes something else happen. An effect is the event or action that happens. The signal words because, so, therefore, and as a result may be used to indicate a cause or an effect. However, not all writers use signal words when relating cause and effect situations. Either the cause or the effect may come first in a passage. One cause may have more than one effect, or one effect may have more than one cause.

Read with students the first part of Chapter X where Douglass describes the incident with the oxen. Have them identify the causes and effects. Suggest that students create their own graphic organizers to depict the causes and effects. Display the organizers and have students explain how their design helps them understand the causes and effects in the book.

Encourage students to think of other cause and effect events in the book so far. You could break the class into small groups, one for each chapter so far, and have students identify cause and effect events in their chapters. Discuss students' findings. Encourage students to create additional cause and effect organizers as they continue reading the book.

LESSON ELEVEN

Objectives
 1. To practice writing to persuade
 2. To bring the book into students' lives
 3. To evaluate students' writing skills

Activity 1
Cause and effect were discussed in the last class meeting, and later in this class time, students will work on writing a persuasive speech. This would be an excellent time to read and analyze one of Frederick Douglass's speeches.

 NOTES: Several collections of Douglass's speeches have been published and are available for purchase. In addition Teacher's Pet Publications offers a copy of Douglass's speech honoring John Brown as a free download (3 MB) from www.tpet.com (on the product page for *Narrative of the Life of Frederick Douglass*). This speech is particularly appropriate for tying together the cause and effect discussions from the previous class meeting as well as being an excellent example of consideration of audience and various means of supporting stated points. *This downloadable speech is actually Douglass's manuscript for the speech as made available from the archives of the Library of Congress, part of a collection of Douglass's documents donated to the National Park Service and passed from that agency to the Library of Congress. Teacher's Pet Publications is not aware of any copyright holders for this manuscript. If one exists, we would definitely like to be contacted with this information (editor@tpet.com).*

Activity 2
Distribute Writing Assignment #2. Discuss the directions in detail and give students the remainder of the class time to work on the assignment. Be sure to let students know when the assignment must be completed, and remember to collect the papers then for evaluation.

 It would be a good practice in public speaking for students to give their speeches orally to the class. Take time to discuss what rules make a good oral presentation, give students a chance to practice, and then set aside a couple of class periods for students to actually give their speeches. Peer evaluations could be beneficial, depending on the personality and skill level(s) of your class.

WRITING ASSIGNMENT #2 *Narrative of the Life of Frederick Douglass*

PROMPT

During his years of slavery, Frederick Douglass longed to be free. Once he became free, he wrote articles and letters and made public speeches advocating freedom for all slaves. Because of Douglass's experiences with slavery, he was passionately committed to fighting against it. Your assignment is to think about your life, choose a topic about which you are passionate, and write a speech persuading your audience to your point of view.

PREWRITING

For some of you, choosing a topic will be easy. Others will have to spend a significant amount of time sorting through ideas to come up with a topic about which you can be passionate. When you find your topic, choose your audience. To whom should you be speaking? What are their characteristics, their views, *their* passions? What can you say and how should you say it to convert them to your way of thinking on this topic? Make a list of things you think will be their objections, things you should acknowledge and discredit, and points that will advance your cause in their eyes. Make notes about sources, examples, statements by others, etc. which will support your ideas. Finally, look at all your notes and organize them into the most coherent and effective order possible.

DRAFTING

Your opening should grab your audience's attention. Whether you use an anecdote, a bold statement, or some other tactic, you need to immediately pull your audience into the topic. The paragraphs that follow should develop your persuasive points in a clear and logical order. Be sure to include effective support for your points and ideas. When you wrap up your speech at the end, clearly summarize your points and leave the audience with a little something to think about: an invitation to join you in the cause, a question or a statement they will remember or think about, or perhaps an applicable quote that sums up your main point.

PEER CONFERENCING/REVISING

When you finish the rough draft of your speech, ask another student to read it. After reading your rough draft, the student should tell you what he/she liked best about your work, which parts were difficult to understand, and ways in which your work could be improved. Reread your text considering your critic's comments, and make the revisions you think are necessary.

PROOFREADING/EDITING

Do a final proofreading of your speech, double checking your grammar, spelling, organization, and the clarity of your ideas.

FINAL DRAFT

Follow your teacher's guidance for completing the final draft of your paper.

LESSON TWELVE

<u>Objectives</u>
1. To read Chapter XI and the Appendix
2. To preview and discuss the study questions and vocabulary for Chapter XI and the Appendix

<u>Activity 1</u>
Divide the class into small groups. Have the groups work together to do the prereading and vocabulary work. Group members can decide how they want to approach the work. Suggest that they may want to assign a few vocabulary words to each member, and have each member teach those vocabulary words to the rest of the group. Or, they may have each member work independently, then gather as a group to go over the vocabulary words.

<u>Activity 2</u>
Tell the students to stay in the same groups as they formed to complete Activity #1. Have them sit in a small circle and take turns reading aloud quietly. As they come to the answer to one of the study questions, they should stop, discuss the question and answer, and write their response.

<u>Activity 3</u>
Have students continue to sit with the same group. Tell each group to choose a spokesperson. Discuss the answers to the study guide questions with the class, having each spokesperson respond for their group.

LESSON THIRTEEN

Objectives
To complete any incomplete assignments

Activity
Take students to the library/media center. Spend a few minutes reviewing the
"correct" answers for the last reading assignment, then give students this class time to
complete their non-fiction assignments or to complete any incomplete writing assignments,
charts, study guides, vocabulary worksheets, etc.

LESSON FOURTEEN

Objectives
To discuss the book at the interpretive and critical levels

Activity
Use the Extra Writing Assignments/Discussions Questions as a springboard for discussing the novel in more depth. Either write answers to the questions on the board or simply have students take notes during the discussion.

NOTE: This is a good time to combine activities to have students practice note-taking skills. If time permits (or if you can make time), allow students to just take notes during the discussion. You should take notes answering the questions on an overhead projector transparency during the discussion, as if you were answering the questions on the board for students to copy. Leave the projector off during the discussion. When the discussion is complete, go back, turn on the projector and briefly review the ideas students should have written into their notes. Allow time for students to fix their notes so they have all the information you want them to have.

If there is extra time, encourage students to ask additional questions.

EXTRA WRITING ASSIGNMENTS/DISCUSSION QUESTIONS *Narrative of the Life of Frederick Douglass*

Interpretive

1. Explain the significance of the title of the book.

2. What are the main conflicts in the autobiography and how are they resolved?

3. Discuss the changes in Frederick Douglass over the course of the book.

4. How does Douglass feel towards his fellow slaves?

5. Douglass believes that slavery is also harmful for the white slave owners. What examples does he give to support his belief?

6. Why is knowledge so important to Douglass?

Critical

7. What effect does the first person narration have on the book?

8. Describe Douglass's writing style. Explain why you do or do not like it.

9. Discuss the imagery used in the book. How vivid is it? How effective is it?

10. Douglass's descriptions of the brutality to the slaves, as well as the sexual treatment of the female slaves by their masters, is quite graphic at times. How does this style affect the reader's understanding of the plight of the slaves?

11. Douglass chose to leave out some details of his escape. How does this influence your overall understanding of his success at escaping? What other details would you like to know?

12. Describe the tone of the autobiography. Discuss how the tone influences the reader's perception of the life of the author.

13. Discuss Douglass's use of irony in the book. Give examples and explain how the irony affects the reader's understanding of slave-slaveholder relationship.

Personal Response

14. Choose one scene from *Narrative of the Life of Frederick Douglass, an American Slave* and write it as a play. Then, explain the difficulties, if any, you encountered in doing so.

15. Explain why *Narrative of the Life of Frederick Douglass, an American Slave* would have been popular to Douglass's audience of abolitionists before the Civil War.

16. *Narrative of the Life of Frederick Douglass, an American Slave* has many difficult or tragic events. Which was the most serious or moving, and why?

17. Did Douglass's experience change the way you look at yourself? How?

18. Did Douglass's experience change the way you look at other people? How?

19. Would you recommend this book to another student? Why or why not?

20. Have you read any other books similar to *Narrative of the Life of Frederick Douglass, an American Slave?* If so, tell about them. Explain how they are similar to and different from Douglass's autobiography.

21. What questions would you like to ask Douglass?

22. What else would you like to know about Captain Anthony, Hugh Auld, or any of the other white slave owners?

23. In Chapter I, Douglass says that the existence of the mulatto children should "do away with the force of the argument, that God cursed Ham, and therefore American slavery is right." These children have white fathers and therefore are not totally black, so slavery "must soon become unscriptural." Explain and respond to this idea.

24. In Chapter XI, Douglass says he does not approve of the underground railroad. What would you say in response to his opinion if you could discuss this issue with him?

25. In the Appendix, Douglass says there are two kinds of Christianity: the slaveholding religion and Christianity proper. Do you agree or disagree with this statement? Explain your reasons.

26. In Chapter II, Douglass compares the slaves who do errands at the Great House Farm with slaves of political parties. Write a response to this statement. Tell why you agree or disagree.

LESSON FIFTEEN

Objectives

1. To discuss selected quotations from the *Narrative of the Life of Frederick Douglass, an American Slave*

2. To discuss students' completed graphic organizers

Activity 1

Read the quotations with students. First ask them to give details from memory about the scene in the book from which the quote came. Then have students check in the book to verify the details. Discuss the importance of the quote. Challenge students to memorize one or more of the quotations and recite it for the class.

Activity 2

Discuss students' completed KWL and cause and effect organizers together in class. Allow time for students to ask questions and make any necessary corrections. Remind students to keep these charts and use them as study aids when they prepare for their test.

You may want to post correctly completed copies of the charts on a bulletin board and/or the class Web site for future reference.

Discuss the significance of the following quotations from *Narrative of the Life of Frederick Douglass, an American Slave.*

1. I have no accurate knowledge of my age, never having seen any authentic record containing it.

2. It was the first of a long series of such outrages, of which I was doomed to be a witness and a participant.

3. They find less difficulty from the want of beds, than from the want of time to sleep; for when their day's work in the fields is done, the most of them having their washing, mending, and cooking to do, and having few or none of the ordinary facilities for doing either of these, very many of their sleeping hours are consumed in preparing for the field the coming day; and when this is done, old and young, male and female, married and single, drop down side by side, on one common bed,--the cold, damp floor,--each covering himself or herself with their miserable blankets; and here they sleep til they are summoned to the field by the driver's horn.

4. The same traits of character might be seen in Colonel Lloyd's slaves, as are seen in the slaves of the political parties.

5. I did not, when a slave, understand the deep meaning of those rude and apparently incoherent songs.

6. I have often been utterly astonished, since I came to the north, to find persons who could speak of the singing, among slaves, as evidence of their contentment and happiness.

7. Colonel Lloyd could not brook any contradictions from a slave. When he spoke, a slave must stand, listen, and tremble; and such was literally the case.

8. They seemed to think that the greatness of their masters was transferable to themselves. It was considered as being bad enough to be a slave; but to be a poor man's slave was deemed a disgrace indeed!

9. I speak advisedly when I say this,--that killing a slave, or any colored person, in Talbot County, Maryland, is not treated as a crime, either by the courts or the community.

10. I was seldom whipped by my old master, and suffered little from any thing else than hunger and cold. I suffered much from hunger, but much more from cold.

11. I shall never forget the ecstasy with which I received the intelligence that my old master (Anthony) had determined to let me go to Baltimore, to live with Mr. Hugh Auld, brother to my old master's son-in-law, Captain Thomas Auld.

12. Going to Baltimore laid the foundation, and opened the gateway, to all my subsequent prosperity. I have ever regarded it as the first plain manifestation of that kind providence which has ever since attended me, and marked my life with so many favors.

13. From my earliest recollection, I date the entertainment of a deep conviction that slavery would not always be able to hold me within its foul embrace; and in the darkest hours of my career in slavery, this living word of faith and spirit of hope departed not from me, but remained like ministering angels to cheer me through the gloom. This good spirit was from God, and to him I offer thanksgiving and praise.

14. The fatal poison of irresponsible power was already in her hands, and soon commenced its infernal work.

15. I now understood what had been to me a most perplexing difficulty--to wit, the white man's power to enslave the black man.

16. Slavery proved as injurious to her as it did to me.

17. Mistress, in teaching me the alphabet, had given me the *inch,* and no precaution could prevent me from taking the *ell.*

18. As I writhed under it, I would at times feel that learning to read had been a curse rather than a blessing. It had given me a view of my wretched condition, without the remedy.

19. At this moment I saw more clearly than ever the brutalizing effects of slavery upon both slave and slaveholder.

20. A great many times have we poor creatures been nearly perishing with hunger, when food in abundance lay mouldering in the safe and smoke-house, and our pious mistress was aware of the fact; and yet that mistress and her husband would kneel every morning, and pray that God would bless them in basket and store!

21. Master Thomas was one of the many pious slaveholders who hold slaves for the very charitable purpose of taking care of them.

22. Mr. Covey's *forte* consisted in his power to deceive.

23. If at any one time of my life more than another, I was made to drink the bitterest dregs of slavery, that time was during the first six months with Mr. Covey.

24. You are loosed from your moorings, and are free; I am fast in my chains, and am a slave.

25. They came because they wished to learn. Their minds had been starved by their cruel masters.

26. We are betrayed!

27. I have found that to make a contented slave, it is necessary to make a thoughtless one. It is necessary to darken his moral and mental vision, and, as far as possible, to annihilate the power of reason.

28. I would keep the merciless slaveholder profoundly ignorant of the means of flight adopted by the slave.

29. I found many, who had not been seven years out of their chains, living in finer houses, and evidently enjoying more of the comforts of life, than the average of slaveholders in Maryland.

30. I could do little; but what I could, I did with a joyful heart, and never felt happier than when in an anti-slavery meeting.

31. I love the pure, peaceable, and impartial Christianity of Christ: I therefore hate the corrupt, slaveholding, women-whipping, cradle-plundering, partial and hypocritical Christianity of this land.

32. Sincerely and earnestly hoping that this little book may do something toward throwing light on the American slave system, and hastening the glad day of deliverance to the millions of my

brethren in bonds--faithfully relying upon the power of truth, love, and justice, for success in my humble efforts--and solemnly pledging my self anew to the sacred cause,--I subscribe myself, Frederick Douglass.

LESSON SIXTEEN

<u>Objectives</u>

1. To practice forming and writing personal opinions
2. To evaluate students' writing skills
3. To consider the book as a whole and how well it accomplished Frederick Douglass's objectives

<u>Activity</u>

Distribute Writing Assignment #3 and discuss the directions in detail. Give students ample time to complete the assignment and tell students when their compositions will be due.

WRITING ASSIGNMENT #3 *Narrative of the Life of Frederick Douglass*

PROMPT
Douglass ends his autobiography with this passage, "Sincerely and earnestly hoping that this little book may do something toward throwing light on the American slave system, and hastening the glad day of deliverance to the millions of my brethren in bonds-faithfully relying upon the power of truth, love, and justice, for success in my humble efforts--and solemnly pledging my self anew to the sacred cause, -- I subscribe myself, Frederick Douglass."
In your opinion, how well does his autobiography do what he hoped? Suppose you were alive in 1845 and read his book. What would your response be to the book?

PREWRITING
Remember that a personal opinion piece should include your thoughts and feelings. As often as possible, support these thoughts and feelings with factual evidence or examples. Make a list of reasons that you think Douglass's autobiography is effective. Organize the list starting with the most important or most convincing reasons first, and proceeding to the least important reason. You may want to do some research on other autobiographies by slaves, or try to find reviews of Douglass's book, or evidence that the book influenced abolitionists of the time.

DRAFTING
Use the first person point of view. Refer to any notes you made during your prewriting time. Write your first draft. Check to make sure you are including your opinion. Use as many descriptive words and images as you can. You may want to use a thesaurus to help you get a variety of words and their exact meanings.

PEER CONFERENCING/REVISING
When you finish the rough draft of your personal opinion piece, ask another student to read it. After reading your rough draft, the student should tell you what he/she liked best about your work, which parts were difficult to understand, and ways in which your work could be improved. Your reader should also be able to summarize your opinion about the effectiveness of Douglass's autobiography. Reread your text considering your critic's comments, and make the revisions you think are necessary.

PROOFREADING/EDITING
Do a final proofreading of your personal opinion piece, double checking your grammar, spelling, organization, and the clarity of your ideas.

FINAL DRAFT
Follow your teacher's guidelines for completing the final draft of your paper.

LESSON SEVENTEEN

Objectives
To review all of the vocabulary work done in this unit

Activity
Choose one or more of the vocabulary review activites below and use your class time as directed.

VOCABULARY REVIEW ACTIVITIES

1. Divide your class into two teams and have an old-fashioned spelling or definition bee.

2. Give individuals or groups of students a Vocabulary Word Search Puzzle for *Narrative of the Life of Frederick Douglass, an American Slave,* along with (or, alternatively, without) a word list. The person (group) to find all of the vocabulary words in the puzzle first wins.

3. Give students a Vocabulary Word Search Puzzle for *Narrative of the Life of Frederick Douglass, an American Slave* without the word list. The person or group to find the most vocabulary words in the puzzle wins.

4. Put a Vocabulary Crossword Puzzle for *Narrative of the Life of Frederick Douglass, an American Slave* onto a transparency on the overhead projector and do the puzzle together as a class.

5. Give students a Vocabulary Matching Worksheet for *Narrative of the Life of Frederick Douglass, an American Slave* to do.

6. Use words from the word jumble page and have students spell them correctly, then use them in original sentences.

7. Have students write a story, newspaper article, or journal entry in which they correctly use as many vocabulary words as possible. Have students read their compositions orally. Post the most original compositions on your bulletin board.

8. Have students work in teams and play charades with the vocabulary words.

9. Have a contest to see which students can find the most vocabulary words used in other sources. You may want to have a bulletin board available so the students can write down their word, the sentence it was used in, and the source.

10. Assign a word to each student, or let students choose a word. Have them look up the origin of the word, the part of speech, definition, a synonym, and an antonym. Then have them write a sentence using the word. Have students present their information orally to the class.

11. Have students work in small groups to create a game using the vocabulary words.

LESSON EIGHTEEN

Objectives
    1. To review the main events and ideas presented in this unit
    2. To prepare for the unit test

Activity
Choose one (or more) of the review games/activities listed below and spend your class time as directed.

REVIEW GAMES/ACTIVITIES

1. Ask the class to make up a unit test for *Narrative of the Life of Frederick Douglass, an American Slave* (including a separate answer key). The test should have 4 sections: multiple choice, true/false, short answer, and essay. Students may use 1/2 period to make the test with a separate answer key and then swap papers and use the other 1/2 class period to take a test a classmate has devised. (open book) You may want to use the unit test included in this packet or take questions from the students' unit tests to formulate your own test.

2. Take 1/2 period for students to make up true and false questions (including the answers). Collect the papers, and divide the class into two teams. Draw a big tic-tac-toe board on the chalkboard. Make one team X and one team O. Ask questions to each side, giving each student one turn. If the question is answered correctly, that students' team's letter (X or O) is placed in the box. If the answer is incorrect, no mark is placed in the box. The object is to get three marks in a row like tic-tac-toe. You may want to keep track of the number of games won for each team.

3. Take 1/2 period for students to make up questions (true/false and short answer). Collect the questions. Divide the class into two teams. You'll alternate asking questions to individual members of teams A & B (like in a spelling bee). The question keeps going from A to B until it is correctly answered, then a new question is asked. A correct answer does not allow the team to get another question. Correct answers are +2 points; incorrect answers are -1 point.

4. Allow students time to quiz each other (in pairs or small groups) from their study guides and class notes.

5. Give students a crossword puzzle for *Narrative of the Life of Frederick Douglass, an American Slave* to complete.

6. Divide your class into two teams. Use the crossword words for *Narrative of the Life of Frederick Douglass, an American Slave* with their letters jumbled as a word list. Student 1 from Team A faces off against Student 1 from Team B. You write the first jumbled word on the board. The first student (1A or 1B) to unscramble the word wins the chance for his/her team to score points. If 1A wins the jumble, go to student 2A and give him/her a clue. He/she must give you the correct word which matches that clue. If he/she does, Team A scores a point, and you give student 3A a clue for which you expect another correct response. Continue giving Team A clues until some team member makes an incorrect response. An incorrect response sends the game back to the jumbled-word face off, this time with students 2A and 2B. Instead of repeating giving clues to the first few students of each team, continue with the student after the one who gave the last incorrect response on the team.

7. Take on the persona of "The Answer Person." Allow students to ask any question about the book. Answer the questions, or tell students where to look in the book to find the answer.

8. Students may enjoy playing charades with events from the story. Select a student to start. Give him/her a card with a scene or event from the story. Allow the players to use their books to find the scene being described. The first person to guess each charade performs the next one.

9. Have individual students draw scenes from the book. Display the scenes and have the rest of the class look in their books to find the chapter or section that is being depicted. The first student to find the correct scene then displays his or her picture. When the game is over, collect the pictures and put them in a binder for students to look at during their free time.

NOTE: If students do not need the extra review, omit this lesson and go on to the test.

LESSON NINETEEN

Objectives
To evaluate students' understanding of the main ideas, themes, and events in *Narrative of the Life of Frederick Douglass, an American Slave*

Activity
Distribute the unit tests. Give students ample time to complete them. Students who finish early may continue to work on Writing Assignment #3 if you have not yet collected the compositions.

Remember to collect the test papers, books, and any other materials you will use again with another class.

NOTE: There are 5 different unit tests included in this LitPlan Teacher Pack. Two are short answer, two are multiple choice. There is one advanced short answer test. The answers to the advanced short answer test will be based on the discussions you have had during class and should be graded accordingly. You should choose the tests and/or test parts which best suit your needs. Matching and short answer tests have answer keys. For essay type questions, grade according to your own criteria based on class discussions and the level of your students. Also, you will need to choose vocabulary words to read orally for the vocabulary sections of the short answer tests.

LESSON TWENTY

Objectives

1. To widen the breadth of students' knowledge about the topics discussed or touched upon in *Narrative of the Life of Frederick Douglass, an American Slave*
2. To present the non-fiction assignments

Ativity 1

Ask each student to give a brief oral report about the non-fiction work he/she read for the non-fiction assignment. Your criteria for evaluating this report will vay depending on the level of your students. You may wish for students to give the complete report without using notes of any kind. Or you may want students to read directly from a written report. You may want to do something between these two options. Make students aware of your criteria in ample time for them to prepare their reports.

Start with one student's report. After that, ask if anyone else in the class has read on a topic related to the first student's report. If no one has, choose another student at random. After each report, be sure to ask if anyone has a report related to the one just completed. That will help keep continuity during the disucssion to the reports.

Activity 2

Collect the students' written reports. Put them in a binder and have the binder available for students to read.

Activity 3

If the class or school has a Web site, post the non-fiction reports there.

UNIT TESTS

Narrative of the Life of Frederick Douglass Short Answer Unit Test 1

I. Matching

_____ 1. ANTHONY

A. Col. who owned the plantation where Douglass first lived

_____ 2. ANNA

B. Slave breaker Douglass eventually beat

_____ 3. BAILEY

C. He escaped slavery and became a great orator.

_____ 4. LLOYD

D. Douglass attributed his good fortune to ___.

_____ 5. DANIEL

E. Lloyd who protected Douglass from older boys

_____ 6. RUGGLES

F. David who helped Douglass in New York

_____ 7. DOUGLASS

G. Name came from the book *Lady of the Lake*

_____ 8. COVEY

H. Douglass's last name at birth

_____ 9. GOD

I. Last name Douglass used in New York

_____ 10. GRANDMOTHER

J. Was cursed in the Bible; slaves supposedly descended from him

_____ 11. HAM

K. Taught Douglass some of the alphabet and spelling

_____ 12. JOHNSON

L. Murdered Douglass's wife's cousin

_____ 13. THOMAS

M. Killed two slaves, one with a hatchet

_____ 14. GORE

N. Douglass's wife

_____ 15. AULD

O. Did not give slaves enough to eat: Master ___

_____ 16. HICK

P. Slave who gave Douglass the root

_____ 17. JENKINS

Q. Cruel; gave severe punishments

_____ 18. LANMAN

R. Douglass's white father, clerk to Lloyd: Aaron ___

_____ 19. FREDERICK

S. She raised Douglass after he was taken from his mother.

II. Short Answer

1. Describe Frederick's relationship with his mother. Include the number of times they saw each other, what their visits were like, and Frederick's age when she died.

2. What are Douglass's observations about this class of mulatto slaves in relation to the south and the American idea of the correctness of slavery?

3. Summarize Douglass's observations about the reasons the slaves usually gave only positive, complimentary comments about their masters.

4. How did Master Daniel Lloyd treat the young Douglass?

5. Compare and contrast the treatment of slaves by the slave owners in the city with the slave owners on the plantations.

6. How old was Douglass when he read "*The Columbian Orator*"? What effect did this book have on him?

7. What regret did Douglass express about the time when he was moved from Master Hugh's home to Master Thomas? Why did he have this regret?

8. Describe the turning point in Douglass's life as a slave that happened when he was with Covey.

9. Master Hugh sometimes gave Douglass six cents of his wages after he had made six dollars, supposedly to encourage him. What effect did this have on Douglass?

10. What newspaper did Douglass begin to read? How did this newspaper affect his ideas and actions?

III. Quotations: Explain the importance and meaning of the following quotations:

1. I have no accurate knowledge of my age, never having seen any authentic record containing it.

2. They seemed to think that the greatness of their masters was transferable to themselves. It was considered as being bad enough to be a slave; but to be a poor man's slave was deemed a disgrace indeed!

3. Slavery proved as injurious to her as it did to me.

4. A great many times have we poor creatures been nearly perishing with hunger, when food in abundance lay mouldering in the safe and smoke-house, and our pious mistress was aware of the fact; and yet that mistress and her husband would kneel every morning, and pray that God would bless them in basket and store!

5. You are loosed from your moorings, and are free; I am fast in my chains, and am a slave.

IV. Composition

1. Compare and contrast Frederick Douglass's life on the Eastern Shore with his life in Baltimore.

2. Frederick Douglass often spoke about cause and effect--the fact that actions and events are the result of something, and those actions and events also have an effect on future events. Using Douglass's own life, give a good example of this concept.

V. Vocabulary

Write the vocabulary words you are given. After writing them down, go back and write in their definitions.

Word	Definition
1	
2	
3	
4	
5	
6	
7	
8	
9	
10	

I. Matching

R	1. ANTHONY	A.	Col. who owned the plantation where Douglass first lived
N	2. ANNA	B.	Slave breaker Douglass eventually beat
H	3. BAILEY	C.	He escaped slavery and became a great orator.
A	4. LLOYD	D.	Douglass attributed his good fortune to ___.
E	5. DANIEL	E.	Lloyd who protected Douglass from older boys
F	6. RUGGLES	F.	David who helped Douglass in New York
G	7. DOUGLASS	G.	Name came from the book *Lady of the Lake*
B	8. COVEY	H.	Douglass's last name at birth
D	9. GOD	I.	Last name Douglass used in New York
S	10. GRANDMOTHER	J.	Was cursed in the Bible; slaves supposedly descended from him
J	11. HAM	K.	Taught Douglass some of the alphabet and spelling
I	12. JOHNSON	L.	Murdered Douglass's wife's cousin
O	13. THOMAS	M.	Killed two slaves, one with a hatchet
Q	14. GORE	N.	Douglass's wife
K	15. AULD	O.	Did not give slaves enough to eat: Master ___
L	16. HICK	P.	Slave who gave Douglass the root
P	17. JENKINS	Q.	Cruel; gave severe punishments
M	18. LANMAN	R.	Douglass's white father, clerk to Lloyd: Aaron ___
C	19. FREDERICK	S.	She raised Douglass after he was taken from his mother.

II. Short Answer

1. Describe Frederick's relationship with his mother. Include the number of times they saw each other, what their visits were like, and Frederick's age when she died.
   Frederick was taken from his mother when he was less than a year old and was then raised by his grandmother. His mother was sent to a farm about twelve miles away to work. He only saw her four or five times in his life. On those occasions, she walked after her workday to the farm where he lived. She put him to bed and then left. She died when he was seven, but he was not permitted to be with her when she was sick or when she died.

2. What are Douglass's observations about this class of mulatto slaves in relation to the south and the American idea of the correctness of slavery?
   Douglass observed that these slaves looked very different from the original African slaves and from the white southerners. He thought their presence might do away with the reasoning that since God cursed Ham, then American slavery was right. Since so many of the slaves were of mixed blood, the reasoning that the descendants of Ham should be cursed would no longer apply.

3. Summarize Douglass's observations about the reasons the slaves usually gave only positive, complimentary comments about their masters.
   The masters had spies among the slaves, and if it was reported that a slave said negative things, the slave could be sold off. Slaves also thought of their own situation as better than that of other slaves. They also thought the greatness of their masters transferred to them.

4. How did Master Daniel Lloyd treat the young Douglass?
   Lloyd protected Frederick from the older boys and shared food with him.

5. Compare and contrast the treatment of slaves by the slave owners in the city with the slave owners on the plantations.
   The slave owners in the city mostly treated their slaves better than the plantation owners did. The slaves in the city had more food, better clothes, and had some privileges.

6. How old was Douglass when he read "*The Columbian Orator*"? What effect did this book have on him?
   He was twelve when he read the book. The book helped him argue against slavery. The book also made him hate the slave owners.

7. What regret did Douglass express about the time when he was moved from Master Hugh's home to Master Thomas? Why did he have this regret?
   He regretted not at least trying to run away, because it was easier to escape from a city than from the country.

8. Describe the turning point in Douglass's life as a slave that happened when he was with Covey.
   The day after Douglass returned to Covey, Douglass resisted as Covey was trying to whip him. Douglass managed to whip Covey, but Covey was not able to hurt Douglass. From this time on, Covey did not again attempt to whip Douglass.

9. Master Hugh sometimes gave Douglass six cents of his wages after he had made six dollars, supposedly to encourage him. What effect did this have on Douglass?
   It made him restless and discontent because it seemed to him an admission that he deserved all of the money.

10. What newspaper did Douglass begin to read? How did this newspaper affect his ideas and actions?
    Douglass began to read the Liberator. *He liked the ideas about anti-slavery and began attending meetings. On August 11, 1841, while attending a meeting at Nantucket, Douglass reluctantly spoke to the group. From then on, he began speaking out against slavery.*

V. Vocabulary

Write the vocabulary words you are given. After writing them down, go back and write in their definitions.

Word	Definition
1	
2	
3	
4	
5	
6	
7	
8	
9	
10	

Select the vocabulary words for Unit Test 1

Narrative of the Life of Frederick Douglass Short Answer Unit Test 2

I. Matching

____ 1.   ANNA   A.   Paper Douglass began reading in New York

____ 2.   BALTIMORE   B.   Douglass's wife

____ 3.   BREAD   C.   Child with slave mother and white father

____ 4.   CAULKING   D.   Location of anti-slavery meeting where Douglass first spoke

____ 5.   LLOYD   E.   He escaped slavery and became a great orator.

____ 6.   COLUMBIAN   F.   Reading *The ____ Orator* helped Douglass argue against slavery.

____ 7.   DANIEL   G.   Lloyd who protected Douglass from older boys

____ 8.   DEVIL   H.   Douglass's mother

____ 9.   GOD   I.   Douglass's age when his mother died

____ 10. HARRIET   J.   Col. who owned the plantation where Douglass first lived

____ 11. LIBERATOR   K.   Douglass lived there with Hugh Auld.

____ 12. GORE   L.   Served by the "slaveholding religion"

____ 13. AULD   M.   Douglass's birthplace

____ 14. MULATTO   N.   Taught Douglass some of the alphabet and spelling

____ 15. NANTUCKET   O.   Cruel; gave severe punishments

____ 16. TUCKAHOE   P.   Douglass attributed his good fortune to ____.

____ 17. SIX   Q.   Number of cents Hugh Auld gave Douglass from his wages

____ 18. SEVEN   R.   Douglass's learned trade, done to ships

____ 19. FREDERICK   S.   Douglass traded it for reading lessons from white boys.

II. Short Answer

1. Where and when was Frederick Douglass born? What was his name at birth? What did he know about his parents?

2. How old was Frederick Douglass when he wrote his narrative?

3. What did Douglass say about the singing of the slaves? How did he feel about the songs?

4. Douglass says that Mr. Gore was "cruel, artful, and obdurate." What are the examples that Douglass gives for each of these adjectives about Mr. Gore?

5. Who were Mr. Thomas Lanman, Mrs. Hick, and Mr. Beal Bondy? What did each of them do? What were the results of their actions?

6. How old was Douglass when he left the Lloyd plantation? Where did he go? With whom did he live there? What was his job?

7. What did Mrs. Auld teach Douglass to do? What did Mr. Auld say when he found out?

8. How old was Douglass when he read "*The Columbian Orator*"? What effect did this book have on him?

9. What regret did Douglass express about the time when he was moved from Master Hugh's home to Master Thomas? Why did he have this regret?

10. Summarize Douglass's thoughts when he looked at the ships on the Chesapeake Bay.

11. According to Douglass, what institution is the "mere covering for the most horrid crimes"? What type of slaveholders are the worst? Why does Douglass think this?

12. How did Douglass feel about the underground railroad?

13. Why did Douglass want to hire himself out, even though Master Hugh took most of the wages?

14. When did Douglass succeed in escaping? Where did he go? How did Douglass feel when he arrived in the free state?

15. What newspaper did Douglass begin to read? How did this newspaper affect his ideas and actions?

III. Quotations: Explain the importance and meaning of the following quotations:

1. It was the first of a long series of such outrages, of which I was doomed to be a witness and a participant.

2. Going to Baltimore laid the foundation, and opened the gateway, to all my subsequent prosperity. I have ever regarded it as the first plain manifestation of that kind providence which has ever since attended me, and marked my life with so many favors.

3. Mistress, in teaching me the alphabet, had given me the *inch*, and no precaution could prevent me from taking the *ell*.

4. Mr. Covey's forte consisted in his power to deceive.

5. I have found that to make a contented slave, it is necessary to make a thoughtless one. It is necessary to darken his moral and mental vision, and, as far as possible, to annihilate the power of reason.

6. I could do little; but what I could, I did with a joyful heart, and never felt happier than when in an anti-slavery meeting.

IV. Composition

1. Compare and contrast two of Frederick Douglass's masters.

2. Which three events in Frederick Douglass's life had the most influence on his achieving his freedom? Explain your choices.

V. Vocabulary

Write the vocabulary words you are given. After writing them down, go back and write in their definitions.

	Word	Definition
1		
2		
3		
4		
5		
6		
7		
8		
9		
10		

I. Matching

B	1. ANNA	A.	Paper Douglass began reading in New York
K	2. BALTIMORE	B.	Douglass's wife
S	3. BREAD	C.	Child with slave mother and white father
R	4. CAULKING	D.	Location of anti-slavery meeting where Douglass first spoke
J	5. LLOYD	E.	He escaped slavery and became a great orator.
F	6. COLUMBIAN	F.	Reading *The* ____ *Orator* helped Douglass argue against slavery.
G	7. DANIEL	G.	Lloyd who protected Douglass from older boys
L	8. DEVIL	H.	Douglass's mother
P	9. GOD	I.	Douglass's age when his mother died
H	10. HARRIET	J.	Col. who owned the plantation where Douglass first lived
A	11. LIBERATOR	K.	Douglass lived there with Hugh Auld.
O	12. GORE	L.	Served by the "slaveholding religion"
N	13. AULD	M.	Douglass's birthplace
C	14. MULATTO	N.	Taught Douglass some of the alphabet and spelling
D	15. NANTUCKET	O.	Cruel; gave severe punishments
M	16. TUCKAHOE	P.	Douglass attributed his good fortune to ___.
Q	17. SIX	Q.	Number of cents Hugh Auld gave Douglass from his wages
I	18. SEVEN	R.	Douglass's learned trade, done to ships
E	19. FREDERICK	S.	Douglass traded it for reading lessons from white boys.

II. Short Answer

1. Where and when was Frederick Douglass born? What was his name at birth? What did he know about his parents?
    He was born in Tuckahoe, near Hillsboro, Maryland. He did not know when he was born but estimated that it was around 1818. His name was Frederick Augustus Washington Bailey. His mother was a slave named Harriet Bailey. He believed that his father was a white man named Captain Aaron Anthony, who owned Harriet Bailey.

2. How old was Frederick Douglass when he wrote his narrative?
    He was about twenty-seven or twenty-eight.

3. What did Douglass say about the singing of the slaves? How did he feel about the songs?
    It was a common belief that slaves sang because they were happy, but this was not true. He said the slaves sang the most when they were unhappy. The songs were a testimony against slavery. Douglass was not able to hear the songs without thinking about the dehumanizing aspects of slavery.

4. Douglass says that Mr. Gore was "cruel, artful, and obdurate." What are the examples that Douglass gives for each of these adjectives about Mr. Gore?
    He was cruel enough to inflict the most severe punishment. He was artful enough to be very tricky. He was obdurate enough to ignore his conscience.

5. Who were Mr. Thomas Lanman, Mrs. Hick, and Mr. Beal Bondy? What did each of them do? What were the results of their actions?
    They were all white slave owners who killed slaves. None of them were convicted since it was not a crime to kill a slave or any other colored person.

6. How old was Douglass when he left the Lloyd plantation? Where did he go? With whom did he live there? What was his job?
    He was about seven or eight when he was sent to Baltimore to live with Mr. Hugh Auld and his family. He was to take care of the Aulds' young son, Thomas.

7. What did Mrs. Auld teach Douglass to do? What did Mr. Auld say when he found out?
    She taught Douglass the alphabet and how to spell some words. Mr. Auld told her to stop. He said that teaching slaves to read made them unmanageable, discontented, and unhappy.

8. How old was Douglass when he read "*The Columbian Orator*"? What effect did this book have on him?
    He was twelve when he read the book. The book helped him argue against slavery. The book also made him hate the slave owners.

9. What regret did Douglass express about the time when he was moved from Master Hugh's home to Master Thomas? Why did he have this regret?
    He regretted not at least trying to run away, because it was easier to escape from a city than from the country.

10. Summarize Douglass's thoughts when he looked at the ships on the Chesapeake Bay.
    He thought it was unfair that the ships were free but he was not free. He vowed to run away. He believed that he was not meant to be a slave forever. He sometimes thought that his misery in slavery would give him more happiness when he was free.

11. According to Douglass, what institution is the "mere covering for the most horrid crimes"? What type of slaveholders are the worst? Why does Douglass think this?
    Religion is the covering; religious slaveholders are the worst. The religious slaveholders professed their religion while mistreating the slaves.

12. How did Douglass feel about the underground railroad?
    He disapproved of the public manner of the system and called it the uppergound railroad. He did not think the system was of much help to the slaves because it made the owners more watchful.

13. Why did Douglass want to hire himself out, even though Master Hugh took most of the wages?
Douglass considered hiring himself out a step toward freedom to be allowed to have the responsibilities of a freeman.

14. When did Douglass succeed in escaping? Where did he go? How did Douglass feel when he arrived in the free state?
He left Baltimore on September 3, 1838. He went to New York. He said it was the highest excitement he ever experienced. He wrote that it was like escaping from a den of hungry lions.

15. What newspaper did Douglass begin to read? How did this newspaper affect his ideas and actions?
Douglass began to read the Liberator. *He liked the ideas about anti-slavery and began attending meetings. On August 11, 1841, while attending a meeting at Nantucket, Douglass reluctantly spoke to the group. From then on, he began speaking out against slavery.*

V. Vocabulary

Write the vocabulary words you are given. After writing them down, go back and write in their definitions.

Word	Definition
1	
2	
3	
4	
5	
6	
7	
8	
9	
10	

Select the vocabulary words for Unit Test 2

Narrative of the Life of Frederick Douglass Advanced Short Answer Unit Test

I. Matching

____	1.	ANTHONY	A. Douglass's last name at birth
____	2.	ANNA	B. Reading *The ____ Orator* helped Douglass argue against slavery.
____	3.	BAILEY	C. David who helped Douglass in New York
____	4.	LLOYD	D. Douglass's mother
____	5.	COLUMBIAN	E. Douglass's white father, clerk to Lloyd: Aaron ___
____	6.	RUGGLES	F. Col. who owned the plantation where Douglass first lived
____	7.	DOUGLASS	G. He escaped slavery and became a great orator.
____	8.	HARRIET	H. Douglass's wife
____	9.	JOHNSON	I. Killed two slaves, one with a hatchet
____	10.	THOMAS	J. Did not give slaves enough to eat: Master ___
____	11.	GORE	K. Last name Douglass used in New York
____	12.	AULD	L. Name came from the book *Lady of the Lake*
____	13.	LANMAN	M. Taught Douglass some of the alphabet and spelling
____	14.	FREDERICK	N. Cruel; gave severe punishments

II. Short Answer

1. Douglass believes that slavery is also harmful for the white slave owners. What examples does he give to support his belief?

2. Why is knowledge so important to Frederick Douglass?

3. Explain why *Narrative of the Life of Frederick Douglass, an American Slave* would have been popular to Douglass's audience of abolitionists before the Civil War.

4. Compare and contrast two of Frederick Douglass's masters.

5. Compare and contrast Frederick Douglass's life on the Eastern Shore with his life in Baltimore.

6. How was Anna an important force in Frederick Douglass's life?

7. Which three events in Frederick Douglass's life had the most influence on his achieving his freedom? Explain your choices.

8. In the Appendix, Douglass says there are two kinds of Christianity: the slaveholding religion and Christianity proper. Do you agree or disagree with this statement? Explain your reasons.

III. Composition
1. Now that you have read, discussed, and become more familiar with Frederick Douglass, what do you think of him? Give a complete answer using what you have learned about him as support for your opinion(s).

IV. Vocabulary
A. Write the vocabulary words you are given. After writing them down, go back and write in their definitions.

Word	Definition
1	
2	
3	
4	
5	
6	
7	
8	
9	
10	

B. Write a short paragraph using 8 of these 10 words.

Narrative of the Life of Frederick Douglass Advanced Short Answer Unit Test Answer Key

I. Matching

E	1.	ANTHONY	A.	Douglass's last name at birth
H	2.	ANNA	B.	Reading *The ____ Orator* helped Douglass argue against slavery.
A	3.	BAILEY	C.	David who helped Douglass in New York
F	4.	LLOYD	D.	Douglass's mother
B	5.	COLUMBIAN	E.	Douglass's white father, clerk to Lloyd: Aaron ___
C	6.	RUGGLES	F.	Col. who owned the plantation where Douglass first lived
L	7.	DOUGLASS	G.	He escaped slavery and became a great orator.
D	8.	HARRIET	H.	Douglass's wife
K	9.	JOHNSON	I.	Killed two slaves, one with a hatchet
J	10.	THOMAS	J.	Did not give slaves enough to eat: Master ___
N	11.	GORE	K.	Last name Douglass used in New York
M	12.	AULD	L.	Name came from the book *Lady of the Lake*
I	13.	LANMAN	M.	Taught Douglass some of the alphabet and spelling
G	14.	FREDERICK	N.	Cruel; gave severe punishments

IV. Vocabulary

A. Write the vocabulary words you are given. After writing them down, go back and write in their definitions.

Word	Definition
1	
2	
3	
4	
5	
6	
7	
8	
9	
10	

Select the vocabulary words for the Advanced Short Answer Test

Narrative of the Life of Frederick Douglass Multiple Choice Unit Test 1

I. Matching

____ 1. ANTHONY   A. Cruel; gave severe punishments

____ 2. ABOLITIONISTS B. Slave breaker Douglass eventually beat

____ 3. ANNA   C. Paper Douglass began reading in New York

____ 4. BALTIMORE   D. He escaped slavery and became a great orator.

____ 5. COLUMBIAN   E. Did not give slaves enough to eat: Master ___

____ 6. RUGGLES   F. Douglass's wife

____ 7. DEVIL   G. Reading *The* ____ *Orator* helped Douglass argue against slavery.

____ 8. COVEY   H. Location of anti-slavery meeting where Douglass first spoke

____ 9. GOD   I. Douglass attributed his good fortune to ___.

____ 10. HAM   J. Douglass moved here from New York: New ___

____ 11. JOHNSON   K. Douglass learned about these anti-slavery people from the newspaper

____ 12. LIBERATOR   L. David who helped Douglass in New York

____ 13. THOMAS   M. Taught Douglass some of the alphabet and spelling

____ 14. GORE   N. Douglass's birthplace

____ 15. AULD   O. Douglass lived there with Hugh Auld.

____ 16. MULATTO   P. Was cursed in the Bible; slaves supposedly descended from him

____ 17. NANTUCKET   Q. Douglass's white father, clerk to Lloyd: Aaron ___

____ 18. BEDFORD   R. Served by the "slaveholding religion"

____ 19. TUCKAHOE   S. Child with slave mother and white father

____ 20. FREDERICK   T. Last name Douglass used in New York

II. Multiple Choice

1. Which sentence about Frederick Douglass is false?
    A. He did not know when he was born but estimated that it was around 1818.
    B. His parents were both slaves on the same plantation.
    C. He was born in Tuckahoe, near Hillsboro, Maryland.
    D. His birth name was Frederick Augustus Washington Bailey.

2. How old was Frederick Douglass when he wrote his narrative?
    A. He was fifty-six.
    B. He was about seventy-one or seventy-two.
    C. He was nineteen.
    D. He was about twenty-seven or twenty-eight.

3. Who was Douglass's first master?
    A. General George Watkins
    B. Mr. Ebenezer Hastings
    C. Reverend Thomas Miller
    D. Captain Aaron Anthony

4. According to Douglass, what kind of comments did slaves usually make about their owners?
    A. Truthful
    B. Nonsensical
    C. Complimentary
    D. Complaining

5. What did Mr. Thomas Lanman, Mrs. Hick, and Mr. Beal Bondy have in common?
    A. They were all white slave owners who were kind and good masters.
    B. Each of them owned Frederick Douglass at some point in his life.
    C. They were all atheists.
    D. They were all white slave owners who killed slaves.

6. Mrs. Auld changed from being a kind, tender-hearted woman to a fierce person with a heart of stone. What made her change?
    A. Her parents died and the grief changed her.
    B. Mr. Auld began to beat her frequently, which changed her personality.
    C. The new preacher she listened to changed her.
    D. The duties of a slave owner changed her.

7. How did Douglass learn to read?
    A. He traded bread for lessons with the poor white boys.
    B. He listened to Mrs. Auld reading her Bible aloud.
    C. Mr. Auld changed his mind and taught Douglass himself.
    D. A worker at the shipyard taught him secretly.

8. When Douglas was twelve he read this book. The book helped him argue against slavery. The book also made him hate the slave owners. What is the title of the book?
    A. The Columbian Orator
    B. Unconstitutionality of Slavery
    C. Dred: A Tale of the Great Dismal Swamp
    D. Uncle Tom's Cabin

9. How did Douglass first begin to learn to write?
    A. By running his fingers over the letters in the Bible
    B. By holding Thomas's hand while he wrote his homework
    C. By copying the letters on the timber at the shipyard
    D. By drawing letters in the air while he was walking

10. Why did Master Thomas send Douglass to live with Edward Covey for a year?
    A. Because Covey had a reputation for being able to train slaves as carpenters
    B. Because Covey had a reputation for being able to break the slaves
    C. Because Covey had a reputation for being able to successfully breed the slaves
    D. Because Covey had a reputation for being able to teach the slaves better manners

11. What happened when Douglass beat Covey?
    A. Douglass realized his mistake and begged for forgiveness.
    B. Covey got even with Douglass later by beating him more frequently after that.
    C. Douglass was immediately sold.
    D. Covey never whipped Douglass again.

12. What happened to Douglass when he got caught during his first attempt to get away?
    A. He was whipped and sent home.
    B. He was sentenced to five years in jail.
    C. Mr. Auld sent him to Baltimore to live with Hugh.
    D. Hugh sent him to work in Alabama.

13. What trade did Douglass learn?
    A. Repairing wagons
    B. Ship caulking
    C. Horse shoeing
    D. Drying tobacco

14. How did Douglass feel about the underground railroad?
    A. He didn't think it was of much help to the slaves because it made the owners more watchful.
    B. He didn't believe in it.
    C. He thought it was just a trap to lure slaves into trouble.
    D. He thought it was a great idea and well-done.

15. What motto did Douglass adopt in the free state?
    A. Don't tread on me!
    B. Give me liberty or give me death!
    C. To thine own self be true.
    D. Trust no man!

III. Composition

1. Why is knowledge so important to Frederick Douglass?

2. What were Frederick Douglass's feelings about religion and faith?

3. How was Anna an important force in Frederick Douglass's life?

4. Which three events in Frederick Douglass's life had the most influence on his achieving his freedom? Explain your choices.

IV. Vocabulary

____ 1.	AUTHENTIC	A.	Totally lacking
____ 2.	IMPERTINENT	B.	Care; watchfulness
____ 3.	CONJECTURE	C.	A person without belief in the religion of the writer
____ 4.	INCOHERENT	D.	Rude; disrespectful
____ 5.	DESOLATE	E.	Guessing
____ 6.	MAXIM	F.	Puzzling; confusing
____ 7.	DEFICIENCY	G.	Genuine; real
____ 8.	SCANTY	H.	Deserted; uninhabited
____ 9.	PERPLEXING	I.	Shocked; horrified
____ 10.	DESTITUTE	J.	Rambling; confused; disjointed
____ 11.	BENEVOLENCE	K.	Less than is needed
____ 12.	APPALLED	L.	Kindness; compassion; good will
____ 13.	AGITATED	M.	Saying; a truth
____ 14.	VIGILANCE	N.	Anxious; nervous
____ 15.	INFIDEL	O.	Lack; shortage

Narrative of the Life of Frederick Douglass Multiple Choice Unit Test 1 Answer Key

I. Matching

Q	1.	ANTHONY	A.	Cruel; gave severe punishments
K	2.	ABOLITIONISTS	B.	Slave breaker Douglass eventually beat
F	3.	ANNA	C.	Paper Douglass began reading in New York
O	4.	BALTIMORE	D.	He escaped slavery and became a great orator.
G	5.	COLUMBIAN	E.	Did not give slaves enough to eat: Master ___
L	6.	RUGGLES	F.	Douglass's wife
R	7.	DEVIL	G.	Reading *The ____ Orator* helped Douglass argue against slavery.
B	8.	COVEY	H.	Location of anti-slavery meeting where Douglass first spoke
I	9.	GOD	I.	Douglass attributed his good fortune to ___.
P	10.	HAM	J.	Douglass moved here from New York: New ____
T	11.	JOHNSON	K.	Douglass learned about these anti-slavery people from the newspaper
C	12.	LIBERATOR	L.	David who helped Douglass in New York
E	13.	THOMAS	M.	Taught Douglass some of the alphabet and spelling
A	14.	GORE	N.	Douglass's birthplace
M	15.	AULD	O.	Douglass lived there with Hugh Auld.
S	16.	MULATTO	P.	Was cursed in the Bible; slaves supposedly descended from him
H	17.	NANTUCKET	Q.	Douglass's white father, clerk to Lloyd: Aaron ____
J	18.	BEDFORD	R.	Served by the "slaveholding religion"
N	19.	TUCKAHOE	S.	Child with slave mother and white father
D	20.	FREDERICK	T.	Last name Douglass used in New York

II. Multiple Choice

B 1.   Which sentence about Frederick Douglass is false?
      A.   He did not know when he was born but estimated that it was around 1818.
      B.   His parents were both slaves on the same plantation.
      C.   He was born in Tuckahoe, near Hillsboro, Maryland.
      D.   His birth name was Frederick Augustus Washington Bailey.

D 2.   How old was Frederick Douglass when he wrote his narrative?
      A.   He was fifty-six.
      B.   He was about seventy-one or seventy-two.
      C.   He was nineteen.
      D.   He was about twenty-seven or twenty-eight.

D 3.   Who was Douglass's first master?
      A.   General George Watkins
      B.   Mr. Ebenezer Hastings
      C.   Reverend Thomas Miller
      D.   Captain Aaron Anthony

C 4.   According to Douglass, what kind of comments did slaves usually make about their owners?
      A.   Truthful
      B.   Nonsensical
      C.   Complimentary
      D.   Complaining

D 5.   What did Mr. Thomas Lanman, Mrs. Hick, and Mr. Beal Bondy have in common?
      A.   They were all white slave owners who were kind and good masters.
      B.   Each of them owned Frederick Douglass at some point in his life.
      C.   They were all atheists.
      D.   They were all white slave owners who killed slaves.

D 6.   Mrs. Auld changed from being a kind, tender-hearted woman to a fierce person with a heart of stone. What made her change?
      A.   Her parents died and the grief changed her.
      B.   Mr. Auld began to beat her frequently, which changed her personality.
      C.   The new preacher she listened to changed her.
      D.   The duties of a slave owner changed her.

A 7.   How did Douglass learn to read?

      A.   He traded bread for lessons with the poor white boys.

      B.   He listened to Mrs. Auld reading her Bible aloud.

      C.   Mr. Auld changed his mind and taught Douglass himself.

      D.   A worker at the shipyard taught him secretly.

A 8.   When Douglas was twelve he read this book. The book helped him argue against slavery. The book also made him hate the slave owners. What is the title of the book?

      A.   The Columbian Orator

      B.   Unconstitutionality of Slavery

      C.   Dred: A Tale of the Great Dismal Swamp

      D.   Uncle Tom's Cabin

C 9.   How did Douglass first begin to learn to write?

      A.   By running his fingers over the letters in the Bible

      B.   By holding Thomas's hand while he wrote his homework

      C.   By copying the letters on the timber at the shipyard

      D.   By drawing letters in the air while he was walking

B 10.   Why did Master Thomas send Douglass to live with Edward Covey for a year?

      A.   Because Covey had a reputation for being able to train slaves as carpenters

      B.   Because Covey had a reputation for being able to break the slaves

      C.   Because Covey had a reputation for being able to successfully breed the slaves

      D.   Because Covey had a reputation for being able to teach the slaves better manners

D 11.   What happened when Douglass beat Covey?

      A.   Douglass realized his mistake and begged for forgiveness.

      B.   Covey got even with Douglass later by beating him more frequently after that.

      C.   Douglass was immediately sold.

      D.   Covey never whipped Douglass again.

C 12.   What happened to Douglass when he got caught during his first attempt to get away?

      A.   He was whipped and sent home.

      B.   He was sentenced to five years in jail.

      C.   Mr. Auld sent him to Baltimore to live with Hugh.

      D.   Hugh sent him to work in Alabama.

B 13.   What trade did Douglass learn?
   A. Repairing wagons
   B. Ship caulking
   C. Horse shoeing
   D. Drying tobacco

A 14.   How did Douglass feel about the underground railroad?
   A. He didn't think it was of much help to the slaves because it made the owners more watchful.
   B. He didn't believe in it.
   C. He thought it was just a trap to lure slaves into trouble.
   D. He thought it was a great idea and well-done.

D 15.   What motto did Douglass adopt in the free state?
   A. Don't tread on me!
   B. Give me liberty or give me death!
   C. To thine own self be true.
   D. Trust no man!

IV. Vocabulary

G	1. AUTHENTIC	A.	Totally lacking
D	2. IMPERTINENT	B.	Care; watchfulness
E	3. CONJECTURE	C.	A person without belief in the religion of the writer
J	4. INCOHERENT	D.	Rude; disrespectful
H	5. DESOLATE	E.	Guessing
M	6. MAXIM	F.	Puzzling; confusing
O	7. DEFICIENCY	G.	Genuine; real
K	8. SCANTY	H.	Deserted; uninhabited
F	9. PERPLEXING	I.	Shocked; horrified
A	10. DESTITUTE	J.	Rambling; confused; disjointed
L	11. BENEVOLENCE	K.	Less than is needed
I	12. APPALLED	L.	Kindness; compassion; good will
N	13. AGITATED	M.	Saying; a truth
B	14. VIGILANCE	N.	Anxious; nervous
C	15. INFIDEL	O.	Lack; shortage

Narrative of the Life of Frederick Douglass Multiple Choice Unit Test 2

I. Matching

____	1.	ANTHONY	A. Douglass learned about these anti-slavery people from the newspaper
____	2.	ABOLITIONISTS	B. Douglass's mother
____	3.	ANNA	C. Reading *The ____ Orator* helped Douglass argue against slavery.
____	4.	BAILEY	D. Taught Douglass some of the alphabet and spelling
____	5.	BALTIMORE	E. Douglass's white father, clerk to Lloyd: Aaron ___
____	6.	LLOYD	F. Paper Douglass began reading in New York
____	7.	COLUMBIAN	G. Killed two slaves, one with a hatchet
____	8.	RUGGLES	H. Cruel; gave severe punishments
____	9.	COVEY	I. Last name Douglass used in New York
____	10.	HARRIET	J. David who helped Douglass in New York
____	11.	JOHNSON	K. Location of anti-slavery meeting where Douglass first spoke
____	12.	LIBERATOR	L. Douglass's birthplace
____	13.	THOMAS	M. Col. who owned the plantation where Douglass first lived
____	14.	GORE	N. Douglass's wife
____	15.	AULD	O. Slave breaker Douglass eventually beat
____	16.	NANTUCKET	P. Did not give slaves enough to eat: Master ___
____	17.	JENKINS	Q. Slave who gave Douglass the root
____	18.	LANMAN	R. Douglass's last name at birth
____	19.	TUCKAHOE	S. Douglass lived there with Hugh Auld.
____	20.	FREDERICK	T. He escaped slavery and became a great orator.

II. Multiple Choice

1.   Which sentence about Frederick Douglass is false?
     A.   He was born in Tuckahoe, near Hillsboro, Maryland.
     B.   His birth name was Frederick Augustus Washington Bailey.
     C.   His parents were both slaves on the same plantation.
     D.   He did not know when he was born but estimated that it was around 1818.

2.   How old was Frederick Douglass when he wrote his narrative?
     A.   He was fifty-six.
     B.   He was nineteen.
     C.   He was about seventy-one or seventy-two.
     D.   He was about twenty-seven or twenty-eight.

3.   The mulatto children had a slave mother but a white father, who was usually the slave owner. Douglass said that these children _____.
     A.   Were often killed at birth if the owner's wife requested it
     B.   Were brought up in the master's house along with his other children
     C.   Were usually treated better than the other slaves
     D.   Were often sold off

4.   Douglass said the slaves sang most when they were ___.
     A.   Unhappy
     B.   Well fed
     C.   Picking cotton
     D.   Happy

5.   Which three words does Douglass use to describe Mr. Gore?
     A.   Uncooperative, moody, and sneaky
     B.   Cruel, artful, and obdurate
     C.   Intelligent, methodical, and selfish
     D.   Irresponsible, sadistic, and grim

6.   When he was about seven or eight, Douglass was sent to Baltimore to live with Mr. Hugh Auld and his family. What was his job there?
     A.   Taking care of the Aulds' young son, Thomas
     B.   Tending the family gardens
     C.   Running errands for Mrs. Auld
     D.   Cleaning the kitchen

7. Mrs. Auld changed from being a kind, tender-hearted woman to a fierce person with a heart of stone. What made her change?
    A. Mr. Auld began to beat her frequently, which changed her personality.
    B. The new preacher she listened to changed her.
    C. The duties of a slave owner changed her.
    D. Her parents died and the grief changed her.

8. What word did Douglass hear that was of interest to him?
    A. Abolitionists
    B. Tubman
    C. Canada
    D. Quaker

9. How did Douglass first begin to learn to write?
    A. By copying the letters on the timber at the shipyard
    B. By holding Thomas's hand while he wrote his homework
    C. By drawing letters in the air while he was walking
    D. By running his fingers over the letters in the Bible

10. Why did Master Thomas send Douglass to live with Edward Covey for a year?
    A. Because Covey had a reputation for being able to break the slaves
    B. Because Covey had a reputation for being able to teach the slaves better manners
    C. Because Covey had a reputation for being able to successfully breed the slaves
    D. Because Covey had a reputation for being able to train slaves as carpenters

11. Douglass thought it was unfair that the _____ were free but he was not free.
    A. Ants on the ground
    B. Birds in the air
    C. Ships on the Chesapeake Bay
    D. Poor white servants

12. What did Covey do to Douglass when he (Douglass) became sick while fanning the wheat?
    A. Covey sent him to the main house to rest.
    B. Covey gave him water and made him go back into the fields.
    C. Covey kicked Douglass in the ribs and hit him in the head with a hickory slat.
    D. Covey took him to a doctor.

13. Another slave named Sandy Jenkins told Douglass to carry _____ on his right side and he would never again be whipped by a white slave owner.

   A. A copper coin
   B. A piece of a certain root
   C. A rabbit's foot
   D. A dried flower

14. What happened when Douglass beat Covey?

   A. Douglass realized his mistake and begged for forgiveness.
   B. Covey never whipped Douglass again.
   C. Douglass was immediately sold.
   D. Covey got even with Douglass later by beating him more frequently after that.

15. According to Douglass, this is the "mere covering for the most horrid crimes."

   A. Prejudice
   B. Love
   C. Religion
   D. Profit

16. Douglass did not give all of the details of his escape because he did not want to embarrass anyone who helped, and what other reason?

   A. He did not want the slaveholders to know how he escaped.
   B. He did not remember all of them.
   C. He was afraid the slave catchers would find him.
   D. He thought each slave should find his or her own way.

17. Master Hugh sometimes gave Douglass six cents of his wages after he had made six dollars, supposedly to encourage him. How did it make him feel?

   A. Worthless
   B. Rich and happy
   C. Eager to work more
   D. Restless and discontented

18. When did Douglass succeed in escaping? Where did he go?

   A. He left Baltimore on November 9, 1840. He went to Canada.
   B. He left Baltimore on July 17, 1837. He went to Philadelphia.
   C. He left Baltimore on December 25, 1841. He went to Kansas.
   D. He left Baltimore on September 3, 1838. He went to New York.

19. What newspaper did Douglass begin to read?
    A. New York Times
    B. Liberator
    C. Anti-Slavery Journal
    D. Underground Railroad Gazette

20. What was the primary characteristic of "slaveholding religion"?
    A. Hypocrisy
    B. Peace
    C. Greed
    D. Truthfulness

III. Composition
1. Name three people who had the strongest influences on Frederick Douglass's life. Explain your choices thoroughly.

2. Now that you have read, discussed, and become more familiar with Frederick Douglass, what do you think of him? Give a complete answer using what you have learned about him as support for your opinion(s).

IV. Vocabulary

_____	1.	ODIOUSNESS	A.		A person without belief in the religion of the writer
_____	2.	DEFILED	B.		Wasteful; extremely extravagant
_____	3.	RAPTURE	C.		Rude behavior
_____	4.	MANIFESTATION	D.		Having one's good name ruined
_____	5.	ABHORRENCE	E.		State of everlasting punishment; hell
_____	6.	DEPRAVITY	F.		Wisdom
_____	7.	EMANCIPATION	G.		Evil; wickedness
_____	8.	VINDICATION	H.		Kindness; compassion; good will
_____	9.	PROFLIGATE	I.		Destroy
_____	10.	SAGACITY	J.		Intense disapproval or dislike
_____	11.	QUAILED	K.		Huge numbers
_____	12.	BENEVOLENCE	L.		Fill
_____	13.	IMPUDENCE	M.		To free from blame
_____	14.	IMBUE	N.		Drew back in fear
_____	15.	PERDITION	O.		Support; justification
_____	16.	ANNIHILATE	P.		Setting free
_____	17.	EXCULPATE	Q.		Equal
_____	18.	MYRIADS	R.		Delight; joy
_____	19.	COMMENSURATE	S.		Being full of hatred
_____	20.	INFIDEL	T.		Expression; revelation; display

I. Matching

E	1.	ANTHONY	A.	Douglass learned about these anti-slavery people from the newspaper
A	2.	ABOLITIONISTS	B.	Douglass's mother
N	3.	ANNA	C.	Reading *The ____ Orator* helped Douglass argue against slavery.
R	4.	BAILEY	D.	Taught Douglass some of the alphabet and spelling
S	5.	BALTIMORE	E.	Douglass's white father, clerk to Lloyd: Aaron ____
M	6.	LLOYD	F.	Paper Douglass began reading in New York
C	7.	COLUMBIAN	G.	Killed two slaves, one with a hatchet
J	8.	RUGGLES	H.	Cruel; gave severe punishments
O	9.	COVEY	I.	Last name Douglass used in New York
B	10.	HARRIET	J.	David who helped Douglass in New York
I	11.	JOHNSON	K.	Location of anti-slavery meeting where Douglass first spoke
F	12.	LIBERATOR	L.	Douglass's birthplace
P	13.	THOMAS	M.	Col. who owned the plantation where Douglass first lived
H	14.	GORE	N.	Douglass's wife
D	15.	AULD	O.	Slave breaker Douglass eventually beat
K	16.	NANTUCKET	P.	Did not give slaves enough to eat: Master ____
Q	17.	JENKINS	Q.	Slave who gave Douglass the root
G	18.	LANMAN	R.	Douglass's last name at birth
L	19.	TUCKAHOE	S.	Douglass lived there with Hugh Auld.
T	20.	FREDERICK	T.	He escaped slavery and became a great orator.

II. Multiple Choice

C 1.   Which sentence about Frederick Douglass is false?

    A.   He was born in Tuckahoe, near Hillsboro, Maryland.

    B.   His birth name was Frederick Augustus Washington Bailey.

    C.   His parents were both slaves on the same plantation.

    D.   He did not know when he was born but estimated that it was around 1818.

D 2.   How old was Frederick Douglass when he wrote his narrative?

    A.   He was fifty-six.

    B.   He was nineteen.

    C.   He was about seventy-one or seventy-two.

    D.   He was about twenty-seven or twenty-eight.

D 3.   The mulatto children had a slave mother but a white father, who was usually the slave owner. Douglass said that these children _____.

    A.   Were often killed at birth if the owner's wife requested it

    B.   Were brought up in the master's house along with his other children

    C.   Were usually treated better than the other slaves

    D.   Were often sold off

A 4.   Douglass said the slaves sang most when they were ___.

    A.   Unhappy

    B.   Well fed

    C.   Picking cotton

    D.   Happy

B 5.   Which three words does Douglass use to describe Mr. Gore?

    A.   Uncooperative, moody, and sneaky

    B.   Cruel, artful, and obdurate

    C.   Intelligent, methodical, and selfish

    D.   Irresponsible, sadistic, and grim

A 6.   When he was about seven or eight, Douglass was sent to Baltimore to live with Mr. Hugh Auld and his family. What was his job there?

    A.   Taking care of the Aulds' young son, Thomas

    B.   Tending the family gardens

    C.   Running errands for Mrs. Auld

    D.   Cleaning the kitchen

C 7.   Mrs. Auld changed from being a kind, tender-hearted woman to a fierce person with a heart of stone. What made her change?

    A. Mr. Auld began to beat her frequently, which changed her personality.

    B. The new preacher she listened to changed her.

    C. The duties of a slave owner changed her.

    D. Her parents died and the grief changed her.

A 8.   What word did Douglass hear that was of interest to him?

    A. Abolitionists

    B. Tubman

    C. Canada

    D. Quaker

A 9.   How did Douglass first begin to learn to write?

    A. By copying the letters on the timber at the shipyard

    B. By holding Thomas's hand while he wrote his homework

    C. By drawing letters in the air while he was walking

    D. By running his fingers over the letters in the Bible

A 10.   Why did Master Thomas send Douglass to live with Edward Covey for a year?

    A. Because Covey had a reputation for being able to break the slaves

    B. Because Covey had a reputation for being able to teach the slaves better manners

    C. Because Covey had a reputation for being able to successfully breed the slaves

    D. Because Covey had a reputation for being able to train slaves as carpenters

C 11.   Douglass thought it was unfair that the _____ were free but he was not free.

    A. Ants on the ground

    B. Birds in the air

    C. Ships on the Chesapeake Bay

    D. Poor white servants

C 12.   What did Covey do to Douglass when he (Douglass) became sick while fanning the wheat?

    A. Covey sent him to the main house to rest.

    B. Covey gave him water and made him go back into the fields.

    C. Covey kicked Douglass in the ribs and hit him in the head with a hickory slat.

    D. Covey took him to a doctor.

B 13.   Another slave named Sandy Jenkins told Douglass to carry _____ on his right side and he would never again be whipped by a white slave owner.

    A. A copper coin

    B. A piece of a certain root

    C. A rabbit's foot

    D. A dried flower

B 14.   What happened when Douglass beat Covey?

    A. Douglass realized his mistake and begged for forgiveness.

    B. Covey never whipped Douglass again.

    C. Douglass was immediately sold.

    D. Covey got even with Douglass later by beating him more frequently after that.

C 15.   According to Douglass, this is the "mere covering for the most horrid crimes."

    A. Prejudice

    B. Love

    C. Religion

    D. Profit

A 16.   Douglass did not give all of the details of his escape because he did not want to embarrass anyone who helped, and what other reason?

    A. He did not want the slaveholders to know how he escaped.

    B. He did not remember all of them.

    C. He was afraid the slave catchers would find him.

    D. He thought each slave should find his or her own way.

D 17.   Master Hugh sometimes gave Douglass six cents of his wages after he had made six dollars, supposedly to encourage him. How did it make him feel?

    A. Worthless

    B. Rich and happy

    C. Eager to work more

    D. Restless and discontented

D 18.   When did Douglass succeed in escaping? Where did he go?

    A. He left Baltimore on November 9, 1840. He went to Canada.

    B. He left Baltimore on July 17, 1837. He went to Philadelphia.

    C. He left Baltimore on December 25, 1841. He went to Kansas.

    D. He left Baltimore on September 3, 1838. He went to New York.

B 19.   What newspaper did Douglass begin to read?

   A. New York Times

   B. Liberator

   C. Anti-Slavery Journal

   D. Underground Railroad Gazette

A 20.   What was the primary characteristic of "slaveholding religion"?

   A. Hypocrisy

   B. Peace

   C. Greed

   D. Truthfulness

IV. Vocabulary

S	1. ODIOUSNESS	A.	A person without belief in the religion of the writer
D	2. DEFILED	B.	Wasteful; extremely extravagant
R	3. RAPTURE	C.	Rude behavior
T	4. MANIFESTATION	D.	Having one's good name ruined
J	5. ABHORRENCE	E.	State of everlasting punishment; hell
G	6. DEPRAVITY	F.	Wisdom
P	7. EMANCIPATION	G.	Evil; wickedness
O	8. VINDICATION	H.	Kindness; compassion; good will
B	9. PROFLIGATE	I.	Destroy
F	10. SAGACITY	J.	Intense disapproval or dislike
N	11. QUAILED	K.	Huge numbers
H	12. BENEVOLENCE	L.	Fill
C	13. IMPUDENCE	M.	To free from blame
L	14. IMBUE	N.	Drew back in fear
E	15. PERDITION	O.	Support; justification
I	16. ANNIHILATE	P.	Setting free
M	17. EXCULPATE	Q.	Equal
K	18. MYRIADS	R.	Delight; joy
Q	19. COMMENSURATE	S.	Being full of hatred
A	20. INFIDEL	T.	Expression; revelation; display

UNIT RESOURCE MATERIALS

BULLETIN BOARD IDEAS *Narrative of the Life of Frederick Douglass*

1. Save one corner of the board for the best of students' writing assignments for *Narrative of the Life of Frederick Douglass, an American Slave*. You may want to use background maps of Maryland, the Northeast, and a map showing the free and slave-holding states in the 1840s to represent the setting of the autobiography.

2. Take one of the word search puzzles and with a marker copy it over in a large size on the bulletin board. Write the clue words to find to one side. Invite students prior to and after class to find the words and circle them on the bulletin board.

3. Have students find or draw pictures that they think resemble the people and scenery in the book.

4. Invite students to help make an interactive bulletin board quiz. Give each student a half-sheet of paper (about 4"x5') folded in half so that it can open. On the outside flap, have each student write a description of one of the characters in the text. On the inside, they will write the name of the character. You can staple or tack these papers to the bulletin board so that the students can read the descriptions and lift the flaps to find the answers.

5. Collect and display pictures of Frederick Douglass and the United States during the slavery era.

6. Display articles about the author, Frederick Douglass.

7. Have each student read one of Frederick Douglass's speeches or letters and summarize it on posterboard with appropriate graphics. Attach the posters to your bulletin board (and save them for the next time you teach this unit!)

8. As an introductory activity, give each student a piece of construction paper and have each one write down a word or a phrase that immediately comes to mind when they think about slavery. Post and discuss each one.

9. As a unit-long activity, have students read personal accounts by or about other slaves. Students should make a poster with graphics displaying the slave's name and a little summary about the person. Stagger the "due dates" so one or two will be added to the bulletin board and briefly discussed each day of the unit.

RELATED TOPICS *Narrative of the Life of Frederick Douglass*

1. Slavery in America
2. Other Famous Orators
3. How To Write And Present A Good Speech
4. The Benefits Of Reading
5. Education
6. How To Achieve Your Dreams/Goals
7. Overcoming Personal Obstacles
8. What Does Freedom Mean?

1. Pick one of the incidents for students to dramatize. Encourage students to write dialog for the characters. (Perhaps you could assign various parts to different groups of students so more than one part could be acted and more students could participate.)

2. Have students design a bulletin board (ready to be put up; not just sketched) for *Narrative of the Life of Frederick Douglass, an American Slave.*

3. Invite someone to talk to the class about the *Narrative* or about slavery in general.

4. Have someone from a civil rights group talk about civil rights in general or civil rights for African Americans in particular.

5. Ask someone from a religious group such as the Friends (Quakers) who were abolitionists to talk to the class about their group's work to help free the slaves.

6. Help students design and produce a talk show. Choose one of the story incidents as the topic. The host will interview the various characters. (Students should make up the questions they want the host to ask the characters.)

7. Have students work in pairs to create an interview with one of the characters. One student should be the interviewer and the other should be the interviewee. Students can work together to compose questions for the interviewer to ask. Each pair of students could present their interview to the class.

8. Invite students who have read other books, articles or speeches by Frederick Douglass to present booktalks to the class.

9. Invite students who have read other books on a similar topic as *Narrative of the Life of Frederick Douglass, an American Slave* to present booktalks to the class. This could include other slave narratives such as those by Olaudah Equiano, Harriet Jacobs, and Phyllis Wheatly.

10. Use some of the related topics (noted earlier for an in-class library) as topics for research, reports, or written papers, or as topics for guest speakers.

11. Invite someone who has lived in one of the areas mentioned in the book to speak to the class.

12. Have students hold small group discussions related to topics in the book. Assign a recorder and a speaker for each group. Have the speaker from each group make a report to the class.

13. In his later years after the *Narrative* was published, Douglass also worked for women's suffrage. Have students research the work he did for women's rights and present a report to the class.

14. Read a book by a more contemporary African American writer such as Alice Walker, Zora Neal Hurston, Richard Wright, or Christopher Paul Curtis. Look for ways that Douglass might have been influential in the author's work. Present your insights to the class.

15. Use the Internet to take a virtual field trip to the site of the places where Douglass lived and worked.

16. Bring in music from the pre-Civil War era, including African American spirituals, and play it for the class.

17. Write additional chapters for the book, telling what happened next in Douglass's life.

No.	Word	Clue/Definition
1.	ABOLITIONISTS	Douglass learned about these anti-slavery people from the newspaper
2.	ANNA	Douglass's wife
3.	ANTHONY	Douglass's white father, clerk to Lloyd: Aaron ___
4.	ARTFUL	Douglass described Mr. Gore as "cruel, ___, and obdurate."
5.	AULD	Taught Douglass some of the alphabet and spelling
6.	BAILEY	Douglass's last name at birth
7.	BALTIMORE	Douglass lived there with Hugh Auld.
8.	BEAL	Shot and killed a slave with a musket: ___ Bondy
9.	BEDFORD	Douglass moved here from New York: New ___
10.	BIRTH	1818 is the estimated year of Douglass's ___.
11.	BREAD	Douglass traded it for reading lessons from white boys.
12.	CAULKING	Douglass's learned trade, done to ships
13.	COLUMBIAN	Reading *The ___ Orator* helped Douglass argue against slavery.
14.	COVEY	Slave breaker Douglass eventually beat
15.	DANIEL	Lloyd who protected Douglass from older boys
16.	DEMBY	Shot by Gore
17.	DEVIL	Served by the "slaveholding religion"
18.	DOUGLASS	Name came from the book *Lady of the Lake*
19.	ESCAPE	It was easier to do this from the city.
20.	FREDERICK	He escaped slavery and became a great orator.
21.	GOD	Douglass attributed his good fortune to ___.
22.	GORE	Cruel; gave severe punishments
23.	GRANDMOTHER	She raised Douglass after he was taken from his mother.
24.	HAM	Was cursed in the Bible; slaves supposedly descended from him
25.	HARRIET	Douglass's mother
26.	HICK	Murdered Douglass's wife's cousin
27.	HIRING	Douglass considered it as a step towards freedom: "___ out"
28.	JENKINS	Slave who gave Douglass the root
29.	JOHNSON	Last name Douglass used in New York
30.	LANMAN	Killed two slaves, one with a hatchet
31.	LIBERATOR	Paper Douglass began reading in New York
32.	LLOYD	Col. who owned the plantation where Douglass first lived
33.	MULATTO	Child with slave mother and white father
34.	NANTUCKET	Location of anti-slavery meeting where Douglass first spoke
35.	RELIGIOUS	Slaveholders of the worst kind had this quality.
36.	ROOT	Supposed to keep slaves from being whipped: lucky ___
37.	RUGGLES	David who helped Douglass in New York
38.	SEPTEMBER	Month of Douglass's final escape

No.	Word	Clue/Definition
39.	SEVEN	Douglass's age when his mother died
40.	SHIPYARD	Douglass worked here when he learned to write.
41.	SINGING	Done when slaves were unhappy, not happy as believed
42.	SIX	Number of cents Hugh Auld gave Douglass from his wages
43.	TAR	Col. Lloyd used it to keep slaves out of the garden.
44.	THOMAS	Did not give slaves enough to eat: Master ___
45.	TIMBER	Douglass copied letters on it to learn to write.
46.	TUCKAHOE	Douglass's birthplace

WORD SEARCH - Frederick Douglass

```
L  R  E  L  I  G  I  O  U  S  J  M  B  J  C  A  J  S  J  M
L  S  P  R  J  Q  B  T  V  N  F  S  A  W  R  N  E  L  O  L
O  A  H  K  T  L  J  A  X  A  R  P  I  M  S  T  N  T  H  J
Y  M  V  Z  U  W  S  B  G  N  E  J  L  R  R  H  K  L  N  K
D  O  U  X  C  D  P  O  V  T  D  J  E  X  Q  O  I  S  S  G
N  H  B  L  K  B  V  L  R  U  E  C  Y  G  B  N  N  J  O  V
C  T  B  Y  A  P  T  I  E  C  R  P  H  F  L  Y  S  X  N  D
G  O  F  C  H  T  N  T  H  K  I  N  T  B  K  L  X  J  K  B
G  C  V  Y  O  M  T  I  T  E  C  T  X  Y  V  V  J  R  A  R
R  G  S  E  E  R  R  O  O  T  K  O  L  R  V  Y  X  L  J  C
M  N  Y  X  Y  E  T  N  M  S  C  D  L  Q  P  T  T  S  V  N
M  I  Y  G  K  B  W  I  D  D  B  M  T  U  S  I  Q  L  J  Y
B  K  S  T  R  M  G  S  N  S  N  R  N  Q  M  M  Y  E  F  K
Q  L  X  H  H  E  W  T  A  F  B  D  E  O  Z  B  D  I  Y  P
L  U  M  M  I  T  N  S  R  V  O  X  R  A  G  E  I  N  L  K
F  A  N  N  A  P  R  U  G  G  L  E  S  L  D  R  S  A  X  B
H  C  N  R  J  E  Y  N  P  O  S  T  S  I  E  C  E  D  N  L
N  J  H  M  Q  S  I  A  K  B  R  L  A  B  M  B  V  G  K  B
L  S  I  V  A  G  L  M  R  E  X  E  L  E  B  E  E  M  C  T
C  G  C  J  N  T  L  G  D  C  C  G  R  Y  S  N  H  G  Z
F  X  K  I  F  S  Y  N  M  F  P  T  U  A  D  C  D  M  M  H
P  B  S  K  J  T  I  Z  J  O  A  L  O  T  C  A  E  D  T  P
P  M  H  D  Z  R  A  L  M  R  S  U  D  O  M  P  V  R  O  D
H  A  R  R  I  E  T  R  K  D  G  I  L  R  X  E  I  W  O  J
H  Y  Q  H  A  R  T  F  U  L  B  G  X  D  C  B  L  P  R  G
```

ABOLITIONISTS	DEVIL	MULATTO
ANNA	DOUGLASS	NANTUCKET
ANTHONY	ESCAPE	RELIGIOUS
ARTFUL	FREDERICK	ROOT
AULD	GOD	RUGGLES
BAILEY	GORE	SEPTEMBER
BALTIMORE	GRANDMOTHER	SEVEN
BEAL	HAM	SHIPYARD
BEDFORD	HARRIET	SINGING
BIRTH	HICK	SIX
BREAD	HIRING	TAR
CAULKING	JENKINS	THOMAS
COLUMBIAN	JOHNSON	TIMBER
COVEY	LANMAN	TUCKAHOE
DANIEL	LIBERATOR	
DEMBY	LLOYD	

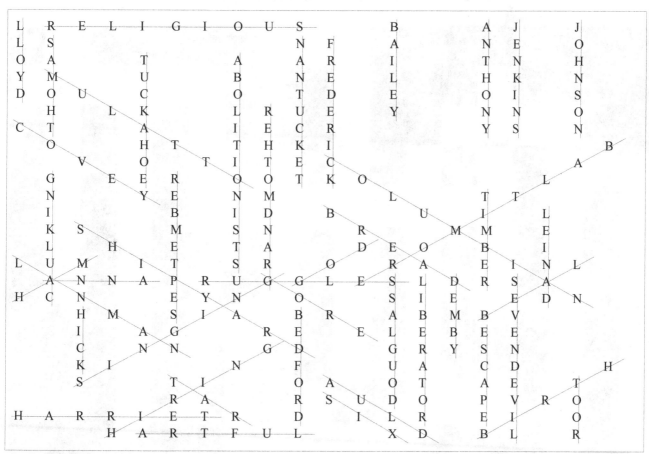

ABOLITIONISTS	DEVIL	MULATTO
ANNA	DOUGLASS	NANTUCKET
ANTHONY	ESCAPE	RELIGIOUS
ARTFUL	FREDERICK	ROOT
AULD	GOD	RUGGLES
BAILEY	GORE	SEPTEMBER
BALTIMORE	GRANDMOTHER	SEVEN
BEAL	HAM	SHIPYARD
BEDFORD	HARRIET	SINGING
BIRTH	HICK	SIX
BREAD	HIRING	TAR
CAULKING	JENKINS	THOMAS
COLUMBIAN	JOHNSON	TIMBER
COVEY	LANMAN	TUCKAHOE
DANIEL	LIBERATOR	
DEMBY	LLOYD	

CROSSWORD - Frederick Douglass

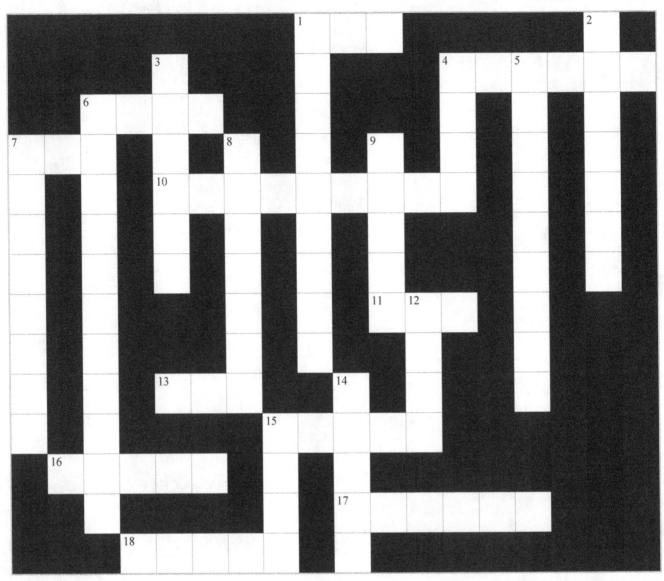

Across

1. Number of cents Hugh Auld gave Douglass from his wages
4. Douglass considered it as a step towards freedom: ___ out
6. Cruel; gave severe punishments
7. The Colonel used it to keep slaves out of the garden.
10. He escaped slavery and became a great orator.
11. Was cursed in the Bible; slaves supposedly descended from him
13. Douglass attributed his good fortune to ___.
15. Douglass traded it for reading lessons from white boys.
16. Shot by Gore
17. This was easier to do from the city.
18. Served by the slaveholding religion

Down

1. Month of Douglass's final escape
2. Douglass's white father, clerk to Lloyd: Aaron ___
3. Douglass described Mr. Gore as cruel, ___, and obdurate.
4. Murdered Douglass's wife's cousin
5. Slaveholders of the worst kind had this quality.
6. She raised Frederick after he was taken from his mother.
7. Douglass's birthplace
8. Douglass moved here from New York: New ___
9. 1818 is the estimated year of Douglass's ___.
12. Taught Douglass some of the alphabet and spelling
14. Douglass's age when his mother died
15. Shot and killed a slave with a musket: ___ Bondy

ANSWER KEY CROSSWORD - Frederick Douglass

Across

1. Number of cents Hugh Auld gave Douglass from his wages
4. Douglass considered it as a step towards freedom: ___ out
6. Cruel; gave severe punishments
7. The Colonel used it to keep slaves out of the garden.
10. He escaped slavery and became a great orator.
11. Was cursed in the Bible; slaves supposedly descended from him
13. Douglass attributed his good fortune to ___.
15. Douglass traded it for reading lessons from white boys.
16. Shot by Gore
17. This was easier to do from the city.
18. Served by the slaveholding religion

Down

1. Month of Douglass's final escape
2. Douglass's white father, clerk to Lloyd: Aaron ___
3. Douglass described Mr. Gore as cruel, ___, and obdurate.
4. Murdered Douglass's wife's cousin
5. Slaveholders of the worst kind had this quality.
6. She raised Frederick after he was taken from his mother.
7. Douglass's birthplace
8. Douglass moved here from New York: New ___
9. 1818 is the estimated year of Douglass's ___.
12. Taught Douglass some of the alphabet and spelling
14. Douglass's age when his mother died
15. Shot and killed a slave with a musket: ___ Bondy

157

_____	1.	ANTHONY	A. Douglass's age when his mother died
_____	2.	JOHNSON	B. Douglass's birthplace
_____	3.	THOMAS	C. Murdered Douglass's wife's cousin
_____	4.	HICK	D. Lloyd who protected Douglass from older boys
_____	5.	NANTUCKET	E. Douglass learned about these anti-slavery people from the newspaper
_____	6.	BEDFORD	F. It was easier to do this from the city.
_____	7.	SEPTEMBER	G. Served by the "slaveholding religion"
_____	8.	TAR	H. Col. Lloyd used it to keep slaves out of the garden.
_____	9.	TUCKAHOE	I. David who helped Douglass in New York
_____	10.	HAM	J. Douglass moved here from New York: New ___
_____	11.	ESCAPE	K. Col. who owned the plantation where Douglass first lived
_____	12.	ABOLITIONISTS	L. Douglass lived there with Hugh Auld.
_____	13.	BALTIMORE	M. Did not give slaves enough to eat: Master ___
_____	14.	CAULKING	N. Douglass's learned trade, done to ships
_____	15.	LLOYD	O. Was cursed in the Bible; slaves supposedly descended from him
_____	16.	DANIEL	P. Douglass's white father, clerk to Lloyd: Aaron ___
_____	17.	RUGGLES	Q. Slave breaker Douglass eventually beat
_____	18.	DEVIL	R. Last name Douglass used in New York
_____	19.	COVEY	S. Location of anti-slavery meeting where Douglass first spoke
_____	20.	SEVEN	T. Month of Douglass's final escape

P	1.	ANTHONY	A. Douglass's age when his mother died
R	2.	JOHNSON	B. Douglass's birthplace
M	3.	THOMAS	C. Murdered Douglass's wife's cousin
C	4.	HICK	D. Lloyd who protected Douglass from older boys
S	5.	NANTUCKET	E. Douglass learned about these anti-slavery people from the newspaper
J	6.	BEDFORD	F. It was easier to do this from the city.
T	7.	SEPTEMBER	G. Served by the "slaveholding religion"
H	8.	TAR	H. Col. Lloyd used it to keep slaves out of the garden.
B	9.	TUCKAHOE	I. David who helped Douglass in New York
O	10.	HAM	J. Douglass moved here from New York: New ___
F	11.	ESCAPE	K. Col. who owned the plantation where Douglass first lived
E	12.	ABOLITIONISTS	L. Douglass lived there with Hugh Auld.
L	13.	BALTIMORE	M. Did not give slaves enough to eat: Master ___
N	14.	CAULKING	N. Douglass's learned trade, done to ships
K	15.	LLOYD	O. Was cursed in the Bible; slaves supposedly descended from him
D	16.	DANIEL	P. Douglass's white father, clerk to Lloyd: Aaron ___
I	17.	RUGGLES	Q. Slave breaker Douglass eventually beat
G	18.	DEVIL	R. Last name Douglass used in New York
Q	19.	COVEY	S. Location of anti-slavery meeting where Douglass first spoke
A	20.	SEVEN	T. Month of Douglass's final escape

____ 1.	ANTHONY	A.	Douglass's last name at birth
____ 2.	ROOT	B.	Reading *The ___ Orator* helped Douglass argue against slavery.
____ 3.	THOMAS	C.	She raised Douglass after he was taken from his mother.
____ 4.	AULD	D.	Served by the "slaveholding religion"
____ 5.	NANTUCKET	E.	Taught Douglass some of the alphabet and spelling
____ 6.	JENKINS	F.	Number of cents Hugh Auld gave Douglass from his wages
____ 7.	SINGING	G.	Douglass considered it as a step towards freedom: "___ out"
____ 8.	TIMBER	H.	Shot by Gore
____ 9.	SIX	I.	Douglass's white father, clerk to Lloyd: Aaron ___
____ 10.	HIRING	J.	Done when slaves were unhappy, not happy as believed
____ 11.	HARRIET	K.	Did not give slaves enough to eat: Master ___
____ 12.	BAILEY	L.	Slave who gave Douglass the root
____ 13.	BREAD	M.	Douglass copied letters on it to learn to write.
____ 14.	COLUMBIAN	N.	Slave breaker Douglass eventually beat
____ 15.	DEMBY	O.	Douglass described Mr. Gore as "cruel, ___, and obdurate."
____ 16.	DEVIL	P.	Douglass traded it for reading lessons from white boys.
____ 17.	COVEY	Q.	Supposed to keep slaves from being whipped: lucky ___
____ 18.	GOD	R.	Douglass attributed his good fortune to ___.
____ 19.	GRANDMOTHER	S.	Douglass's mother
____ 20.	ARTFUL	T.	Location of anti-slavery meeting where Douglass first spoke

I	1. ANTHONY		A.	Douglass's last name at birth
Q	2. ROOT		B.	Reading *The ___ Orator* helped Douglass argue against slavery.
K	3. THOMAS		C.	She raised Douglass after he was taken from his mother.
E	4. AULD		D.	Served by the "slaveholding religion"
T	5. NANTUCKET		E.	Taught Douglass some of the alphabet and spelling
L	6. JENKINS		F.	Number of cents Hugh Auld gave Douglass from his wages
J	7. SINGING		G.	Douglass considered it as a step towards freedom: "___ out"
M	8. TIMBER		H.	Shot by Gore
F	9. SIX		I.	Douglass's white father, clerk to Lloyd: Aaron ___
G	10. HIRING		J.	Done when slaves were unhappy, not happy as believed
S	11. HARRIET		K.	Did not give slaves enough to eat: Master ___
A	12. BAILEY		L.	Slave who gave Douglass the root
P	13. BREAD		M.	Douglass copied letters on it to learn to write.
B	14. COLUMBIAN		N.	Slave breaker Douglass eventually beat
H	15. DEMBY		O.	Douglass described Mr. Gore as "cruel, ___, and obdurate."
D	16. DEVIL		P.	Douglass traded it for reading lessons from white boys.
N	17. COVEY		Q.	Supposed to keep slaves from being whipped: lucky ___
R	18. GOD		R.	Douglass attributed his good fortune to ___.
C	19. GRANDMOTHER		S.	Douglass's mother
O	20. ARTFUL		T.	Location of anti-slavery meeting where Douglass first spoke

_____ = 1. NNAA
Douglass's wife

_____ = 2. GEOR
Cruel; gave severe punishments

_____ = 3. OTUAMLT
Child with slave mother and white father

_____ = 4. LUIIGOSRE
Slaveholders of the worst kind had this quality.

_____ = 5. EPETEBSMR
Month of Douglass's final escape

_____ = 6. SIHPAYDR
Douglass worked here when he learned to write.

_____ = 7. MANALN
Killed two slaves, one with a hatchet

_____ = 8. TAEOHCUK
Douglass's birthplace

_____ = 9. RITHB
1818 is the estimated year of Douglass's ___.

_____ = 10. IETBLAROR
Paper Douglass began reading in New York

_____ = 11. NNSOOJH
Last name Douglass used in New York

_____ = 12. BAEL
Shot and killed a slave with a musket: ___ Bondy

_____ = 13. AICNLKGU
Douglass's learned trade, done to ships

_____ = 14. LOLYD
Col. who owned the plantation where Douglass first lived

_____ = 15. NOBCLIMUA
Reading The ___ Orator helped Douglass argue against slavery.

_____ = 16. GUGRLSE
David who helped Douglass in New York

_____ = 17. SLSAOUDG
Name came from the book *Lady of the Lake*

_____ = 18. CEPSAE
It was easier to do this from the city.

_____ = 19. HRAETRI
Douglass's mother

_____ = 20. RIDCREKFE
He escaped slavery and became a great orator.

ANNA   = 1.   NNAA
Douglass's wife

GORE   = 2.   GEOR
Cruel; gave severe punishments

MULATTO   = 3.   OTUAMLT
Child with slave mother and white father

RELIGIOUS   = 4.   LUIIGOSRE
Slaveholders of the worst kind had this quality.

SEPTEMBER   = 5.   EPETEBSMR
Month of Douglass's final escape

SHIPYARD   = 6.   SIHPAYDR
Douglass worked here when he learned to write.

LANMAN   = 7.   MANALN
Killed two slaves, one with a hatchet

TUCKAHOE   = 8.   TAEOHCUK
Douglass's birthplace

BIRTH   = 9.   RITHB
1818 is the estimated year of Douglass's ___.

LIBERATOR   = 10.   IETBLAROR
Paper Douglass began reading in New York

JOHNSON   = 11.   NNSOOJH
Last name Douglass used in New York

BEAL   = 12.   BAEL
Shot and killed a slave with a musket: ___ Bondy

CAULKING   = 13.   AICNLKGU
Douglass's learned trade, done to ships

LLOYD   = 14.   LOLYD
Col. who owned the plantation where Douglass first lived

COLUMBIAN   = 15.   NOBCLIMUA
Reading *The ___ Orator* helped Douglass argue against slavery.

RUGGLES   = 16.   GUGRLSE
David who helped Douglass in New York

DOUGLASS   = 17.   SLSAOUDG
Name came from the book *Lady of the Lake*

ESCAPE   = 18.   CEPSAE
It was easier to do this from the city.

HARRIET   = 19.   HRAETRI
Douglass's mother

FREDERICK   = 20.   RIDCREKFE
He escaped slavery and became a great orator.

_____ = 1. LOASISITINOBT
Douglass learned about these anti-slavery people from the newspaper

_____ = 2. UDAL
Taught Douglass some of the alphabet and spelling

_____ = 3. TEATKUCNN
Location of anti-slavery meeting where Douglass first spoke

_____ = 4. RELGOSIIU
Slaveholders of the worst kind had this quality.

_____ = 5. IEKNJSN
Slave who gave Douglass the root

_____ = 6. IRDYHPSA
Douglass worked here when he learned to write.

_____ = 7. MNLANA
Killed two slaves, one with a hatchet

_____ = 8. EBIMRT
Douglass copied letters on it to learn to write.

_____ = 9. KEIRDFECR
He escaped slavery and became a great orator.

_____ = 10. SHAOMT
Did not give slaves enough to eat: Master ___

_____ = 11. OILTEARRB
Paper Douglass began reading in New York

_____ = 12. BIYELA
Douglass's last name at birth

_____ = 13. RLIEAOTMB
Douglass lived there with Hugh Auld.

_____ = 14. ACLMUBINO
Reading *The ___ Orator* helped Douglass argue against slavery.

_____ = 15. LSSGDUOA
Name came from the book *Lady of the Lake*

_____ = 16. DHEGMARRNOT
She raised Douglass after he was taken from his mother.

_____ = 17. TEIRAHR
Douglass's mother

_____ = 18. IHRGIN
Douglass considered it as a step towards freedom: "___ out"

_____ = 19. NJOSOHN
Last name Douglass used in New York

_____ = 20. LUARTF
Douglass described Mr. Gore as "cruel, ___, and obdurate."

ABOLITIONISTS = 1. LOASISITINOBT
Douglass learned about these anti-slavery people from the newspaper

AULD = 2. UDAL
Taught Douglass some of the alphabet and spelling

NANTUCKET = 3. TEATKUCNN
Location of anti-slavery meeting where Douglass first spoke

RELIGIOUS = 4. RELGOSIIU
Slaveholders of the worst kind had this quality.

JENKINS = 5. IEKNJSN
Slave who gave Douglass the root

SHIPYARD = 6. IRDYHPSA
Douglass worked here when he learned to write.

LANMAN = 7. MNLANA
Killed two slaves, one with a hatchet

TIMBER = 8. EBIMRT
Douglass copied letters on it to learn to write.

FREDERICK = 9. KEIRDFECR
He escaped slavery and became a great orator.

THOMAS = 10. SHAOMT
Did not give slaves enough to eat: Master ___

LIBERATOR = 11. OILTEARRB
Paper Douglass began reading in New York

BAILEY = 12. BIYELA
Douglass's last name at birth

BALTIMORE = 13. RLIEAOTMB
Douglass lived there with Hugh Auld.

COLUMBIAN = 14. ACLMUBINO
Reading *The ___ Orator* helped Douglass argue against slavery.

DOUGLASS = 15. LSSGDUOA
Name came from the book *Lady of the Lake*

GRANDMOTHER = 16. DHEGMARRNOT
She raised Douglass after he was taken from his mother.

HARRIET = 17. TEIRAHR
Douglass's mother

HIRING = 18. IHRGIN
Douglass considered it as a step towards freedom: "___ out"

JOHNSON = 19. NJOSOHN
Last name Douglass used in New York

ARTFUL = 20. LUARTF
Douglass described Mr. Gore as "cruel, ___, and obdurate."

VOCABULARY RESOURCE MATERIALS

Narrative of the Life of Frederick Douglass Vocabulary

No.	Word	Clue/Definition
1.	ABHORRENCE	Intense disapproval or dislike
2.	AGITATED	Anxious; nervous
3.	ANNIHILATE	Destroy
4.	APPALLED	Shocked; horrified
5.	ARDENTLY	Enthusiastically
6.	AUTHENTIC	Genuine; real
7.	AVAILED	Made useful; helped
8.	BENEVOLENCE	Kindness; compassion; good will
9.	CENSURED	Severely criticized
10.	COMMENSURATE	Equal
11.	CONJECTURE	Guessing
12.	CONSUMMATE	Complete
13.	DEFICIENCY	Lack; shortage
14.	DEFILED	Having one's good name ruined
15.	DENUNCIATION	Condemnation; criticism
16.	DEPRAVITY	Evil; wickedness
17.	DESOLATE	Deserted; uninhabited
18.	DESTITUTE	Totally lacking
19.	DETESTATION	Hatred; loathing
20.	EMANCIPATION	Setting free
21.	EXCULPATE	To free from blame
22.	EXHORTED	Urged; insisted
23.	IMBIBED	Took into the mind; absorbed
24.	IMBUE	Fill
25.	IMMUTABLE	Not changeable
26.	IMPERTINENT	Rude; disrespectful
27.	IMPUDENCE	Rude behavior
28.	IMPUTATIONS	Accusations
29.	INCOHERENT	Rambling; confused; disjointed
30.	INFIDEL	A person without belief in the religion of the writer
31.	MANIFESTATION	Expression; revelation; display
32.	MAXIM	Saying; a truth
33.	MYRIADS	Huge numbers
34.	OBDURATE	Stubborn
35.	ODIOUSNESS	Being full of hatred
36.	PERDITION	State of everlasting punishment; hell
37.	PERNICIOUS	Destructive; harmful
38.	PERPLEXING	Puzzling; confusing
39.	PROFLIGATE	Wasteful; extremely extravagant

No.	Word	Clue/Definition
40.	PROVIDENCE	Care or guardianship exercised by a deity
41.	QUAILED	Drew back in fear
42.	RAPTURE	Delight; joy
43.	RETALIATION	Revenge; getting even
44.	SAGACITY	Wisdom
45.	SCANTY	Less than is needed
46.	SCATHING	Scornful; mocking
47.	SUNDERED	Separated
48.	VIGILANCE	Care; watchfulness
49.	VINDICATION	Support; justification

VOCABULARY WORD SEARCH - Frederick Douglass

```
A B H O R R E N C E R E T A P L U C X E
G A Z M T B T D C B E A D T V D N F Y X
I P P N S L U E L Q T A P E M A V W Z L
T P E H A T T P D N A O U T F Y I P Y I
A A R C G N I R S L L I B T U I T L M H
T L N O A E T A C C I V M D H R L P E K
E L I N C R S V A M A M L B U E E E H D
D E C S I E I N A T T Y D I R N V D S
E D I U T H D T T X I S H R T B A T F S P
R B O M Y O I Y Y I O L K I I Q E T I D
U E U M M C Y L J M N L N Q N A Z D E C
S N S A Z N Y S A C T E W U M G D H Y Z
N E E T N I J P L T N Y K A P D I S F G
E V M E D H D D N T E P N I E E M S Q F
C O A C E J Q Z E C B I H L R S M N B N
Y L N T L L P Y F F V Y E P O U O M R
Q E C A E V E G E E I V Q D L L T I A V
G N I L S B Q X S R X C T F E A A T R Z
M C P I T K G T H Y D R I P X T B A D R
Q E A G A W A B S O R I Z E I E L T E D
G K T I T Z Z D F R R T Q N Y E U N J
V Q I V I N F I D E L T G I G C B P T K
V C O O O M S U N D E R E D O M Y M L R
D E N U N C I A T I O N C D I N Q I Y X
```

ABHORRENCE	DESOLATE	MAXIM
AGITATED	DESTITUTE	MYRIADS
ANNIHILATE	DETESTATION	OBDURATE
APPALLED	EMANCIPATION	PERDITION
ARDENTLY	EXCULPATE	PERNICIOUS
AUTHENTIC	EXHORTED	PERPLEXING
AVAILED	IMBIBED	QUAILED
BENEVOLENCE	IMBUE	RAPTURE
CENSURED	IMMUTABLE	RETALIATION
CONSUMMATE	IMPERTINENT	SAGACITY
DEFICIENCY	IMPUTATIONS	SCANTY
DEFILED	INCOHERENT	SCATHING
DENUNCIATION	INFIDEL	SUNDERED
DEPRAVITY	MANIFESTATION	VIGILANCE

171

```
A  B  H  O  R  R  E  N  C  E  R  E  T  A  P  L  U  C  X  E
G  A        T     D           E     A  D     V
I  P  P     S     U           E     A  P  E     A
T  P  E     A  T  T     P     L  I  B  T  U  I     L  M  I
A  A  R  C  G  N  I  R  R  S  C  C     M  D  H  R  L  P  E
T  L  N  O  A  N  T  E  V  A  C  I  M  B  U  E  E  E     D
E  L  I  C  N  E  S  V  I  M  A  A  T  Y  I  R  N  R     D
D  I  C  I  T  R  E  D  T  I  X  T  I     H  R  T  B  A  T
E  B  O  U  E  R  H  D  Y  Y  I  O  I     R  N  A     D  I
R  E  U  M  R  H  O  I  A  I  M  N        I  Q  A     D  E  C
U  N  S  M  Y  O  I  C  L  O  N     N     N  U  M  G  D  S
S  E  E  A     I  Y  N  A     M  E        A  P  D  I  S
N  E  M  T        L     T  N     N     I  L  E  M  S  N
E  V  A  C     D  A     T  E     N  I  E  R  S  M  N  O  I
C  O  N  D  E  E  T     I        L  I  E  P  O  U  I  A  R
   L  C  E  P  E  F  F     C     E  E  X  O  L  T  I  D
   E  I  T  E  X  E  R  I  D  I     X  D  A  A  T  A  E  N
   N  P  A  A  S  R  C  T     I  E  I  E  L  B  L  T  T
   C  A  T  T     I  O  R  D  I  N  G  L  C  B  U  P  L
   E  T  I        O  O  I  T     I  G  C  B  Y  M  I  Y
   I  V  T     T  I  N  F  I  D  E  L  O  M  Y  M  I
   O  O  O        S  U  N  D  E  R  E  D  O  M  I  I  Y
D  E  N  U  N  C  I  A  T  I  O  N           D  I  N
```

ABHORRENCE   DESOLATE   MAXIM

AGITATED   DESTITUTE   MYRIADS

ANNIHILATE   DETESTATION   OBDURATE

APPALLED   EMANCIPATION   PERDITION

ARDENTLY   EXCULPATE   PERNICIOUS

AUTHENTIC   EXHORTED   PERPLEXING

AVAILED   IMBIBED   QUAILED

BENEVOLENCE   IMBUE   RAPTURE

CENSURED   IMMUTABLE   RETALIATION

CONSUMMATE   IMPERTINENT   SAGACITY

DEFICIENCY   IMPUTATIONS   SCANTY

DEFILED   INCOHERENT   SCATHING

DENUNCIATION   INFIDEL   SUNDERED

DEPRAVITY   MANIFESTATION   VIGILANCE

VOCABULARY CROSSWORD - Frederick Douglass

Across
1. Shocked; horrified
3. Not changeable
5. Huge numbers
6. Having one's good name ruined
9. Hatred; loathing
12. To free from blame
14. Took into the mind; absorbed
16. Delight; joy
17. Expression; revelation; display
18. Kindness; compassion; good will

Down
2. Destructive; harmful
3. Fill
4. Anxious; nervous
7. Destroy
8. Lack; shortage
9. Evil; wickedness
10. Less than is needed
11. Rude behavior
13. Stubborn
15. Saying; a truth

ANSWER KEY VOCABULARY CROSSWORD - Frederick Douglass

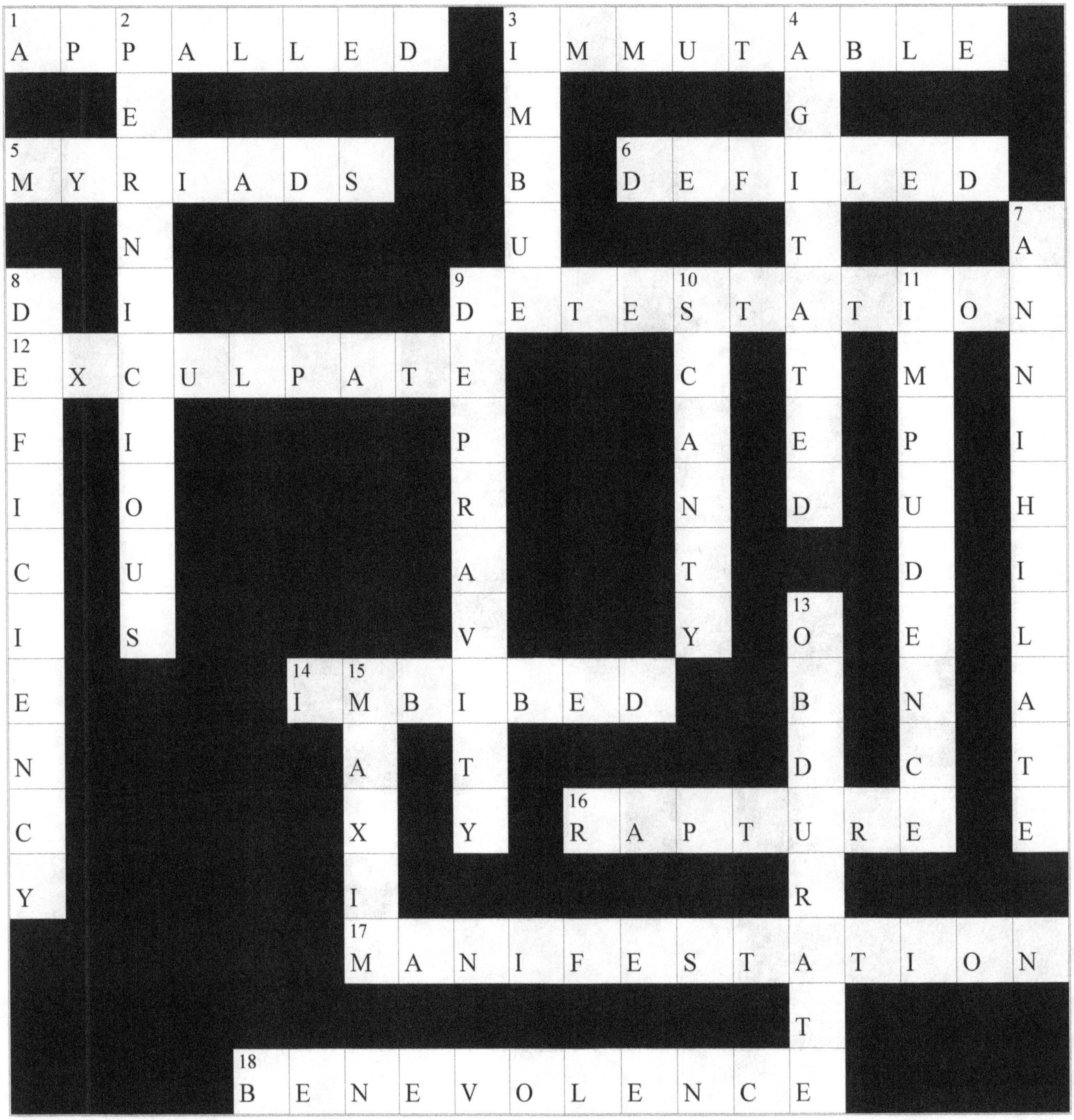

(Completed crossword grid answers)

Across:
1. APPALLED
3. IMMUTABLE
5. MYRIADS
6. DEFILED
9. DETESTATION
12. EXCULPATE
14. IMBIBED
16. RAPTURE
17. MANIFESTATION
18. BENEVOLENCE

Down:
2. PERNICIOUS
3. IMBUE
4. AGITATED
7. ANNIHILATE
8. DEFICIENCY
9. DEPRAVITY
10. SCANTY
11. IMPUDENCE
13. OBDURATE
15. MAXIM

Across
1. Shocked; horrified
3. Not changeable
5. Huge numbers
6. Having one's good name ruined
9. Hatred; loathing
12. To free from blame
14. Took into the mind; absorbed
16. Delight; joy
17. Expression; revelation; display
18. Kindness; compassion; good will

Down
2. Destructive; harmful
3. Fill
4. Anxious; nervous
7. Destroy
8. Lack; shortage
9. Evil; wickedness
10. Less than is needed
11. Rude behavior
13. Stubborn
15. Saying; a truth

VOCABULARY MATCHING 1 *Narrative of the Life of Frederick Douglass*

____ 1. ANNIHILATE

____ 2. PERDITION

____ 3. PERPLEXING

____ 4. PROFLIGATE

____ 5. QUAILED

____ 6. RAPTURE

____ 7. SAGACITY

____ 8. SCANTY

____ 9. VIGILANCE

____ 10. MYRIADS

____ 11. INFIDEL

____ 12. AUTHENTIC

____ 13. CENSURED

____ 14. CONSUMMATE

____ 15. DENUNCIATION

____ 16. DESTITUTE

____ 17. EXCULPATE

____ 18. IMBUE

____ 19. IMPUDENCE

____ 20. VINDICATION

A. Rude behavior

B. Totally lacking

C. Wasteful; extremely extravagant

D. Genuine; real

E. Huge numbers

F. Delight; joy

G. Fill

H. Puzzling; confusing

I. A person without belief in the religion of the writer

J. Wisdom

K. Care; watchfulness

L. Severely criticized

M. Condemnation; criticism

N. To free from blame

O. Less than is needed

P. State of everlasting punishment; hell

Q. Drew back in fear

R. Support; justification

S. Complete

T. Destroy

T	1.	ANNIHILATE	A.	Rude behavior
P	2.	PERDITION	B.	Totally lacking
H	3.	PERPLEXING	C.	Wasteful; extremely extravagant
C	4.	PROFLIGATE	D.	Genuine; real
Q	5.	QUAILED	E.	Huge numbers
F	6.	RAPTURE	F.	Delight; joy
J	7.	SAGACITY	G.	Fill
O	8.	SCANTY	H.	Puzzling; confusing
K	9.	VIGILANCE	I.	A person without belief in the religion of the writer
E	10.	MYRIADS	J.	Wisdom
I	11.	INFIDEL	K.	Care; watchfulness
D	12.	AUTHENTIC	L.	Severely criticized
L	13.	CENSURED	M.	Condemnation; criticism
S	14.	CONSUMMATE	N.	To free from blame
M	15.	DENUNCIATION	O.	Less than is needed
B	16.	DESTITUTE	P.	State of everlasting punishment; hell
N	17.	EXCULPATE	Q.	Drew back in fear
G	18.	IMBUE	R.	Support; justification
A	19.	IMPUDENCE	S.	Complete
R	20.	VINDICATION	T.	Destroy

____ 1.	AGITATED	A.	Not changeable
____ 2.	IMPERTINENT	B.	Being full of hatred
____ 3.	INCOHERENT	C.	Saying; a truth
____ 4.	MANIFESTATION	D.	Destructive; harmful
____ 5.	MAXIM	E.	Guessing
____ 6.	ODIOUSNESS	F.	Enthusiastically
____ 7.	PERNICIOUS	G.	Evil; wickedness
____ 8.	RAPTURE	H.	Having one's good name ruined
____ 9.	SCANTY	I.	Rambling; confused; disjointed
____ 10.	IMMUTABLE	J.	Expression; revelation; display
____ 11.	IMBIBED	K.	Kindness; compassion; good will
____ 12.	ARDENTLY	L.	Hatred; loathing
____ 13.	BENEVOLENCE	M.	Separated
____ 14.	CONJECTURE	N.	Less than is needed
____ 15.	DEFILED	O.	Setting free
____ 16.	DEPRAVITY	P.	Delight; joy
____ 17.	DESOLATE	Q.	Took into the mind; absorbed
____ 18.	DETESTATION	R.	Rude; disrespectful
____ 19.	EMANCIPATION	S.	Deserted; uninhabited
____ 20.	SUNDERED	T.	Anxious; nervous

T	1. AGITATED	A.	Not changeable
R	2. IMPERTINENT	B.	Being full of hatred
I	3. INCOHERENT	C.	Saying; a truth
J	4. MANIFESTATION	D.	Destructive; harmful
C	5. MAXIM	E.	Guessing
B	6. ODIOUSNESS	F.	Enthusiastically
D	7. PERNICIOUS	G.	Evil; wickedness
P	8. RAPTURE	H.	Having one's good name ruined
N	9. SCANTY	I.	Rambling; confused; disjointed
A	10. IMMUTABLE	J.	Expression; revelation; display
Q	11. IMBIBED	K.	Kindness; compassion; good will
F	12. ARDENTLY	L.	Hatred; loathing
K	13. BENEVOLENCE	M.	Separated
E	14. CONJECTURE	N.	Less than is needed
H	15. DEFILED	O.	Setting free
G	16. DEPRAVITY	P.	Delight; joy
S	17. DESOLATE	Q.	Took into the mind; absorbed
L	18. DETESTATION	R.	Rude; disrespectful
O	19. EMANCIPATION	S.	Deserted; uninhabited
M	20. SUNDERED	T.	Anxious; nervous

_____ = 1. ARCBNEHROE
Intense disapproval or dislike

_____ = 2. ENUSODSSIO
Being full of hatred

_____ = 3. OIENPRITD
State of everlasting punishment; hell

_____ = 4. EGXILPPENR
Puzzling; confusing

_____ = 5. GOERFITLPA
Wasteful; extremely extravagant

_____ = 6. EIRPNDOCVE
Care or guardianship exercised by a deity

_____ = 7. IIRTTOLNAAE
Revenge; getting even

_____ = 8. NYTCAS
Less than is needed

_____ = 9. DESURNED
Separated

_____ = 10. NSMTNOIAIFTEA
Expression; revelation; display

_____ = 11. HEORICNTEN
Rambling; confused; disjointed

_____ = 12. IILETNHANA
Destroy

_____ = 13. LVBEONEECNE
Kindness; compassion; good will

_____ = 14. ACTSEUORMMEN
Equal

_____ = 15. MSANUOETMC
Complete

_____ = 16. UOIAENCINNTD
Condemnation; criticism

_____ = 17. TAANOPICNIME
Setting free

_____ = 18. LEPXTAEUC
To free from blame

_____ = 19. INPTMRIEENT
Rude; disrespectful

_____ = 20. AINNDICOTIV
Support; justification

ABHORRENCE = 1. ARCBNEHROE
Intense disapproval or dislike

ODIOUSNESS = 2. ENUSODSSIO
Being full of hatred

PERDITION = 3. OIENPRITD
State of everlasting punishment; hell

PERPLEXING = 4. EGXILPPENR
Puzzling; confusing

PROFLIGATE = 5. GOERFITLPA
Wasteful; extremely extravagant

PROVIDENCE = 6. EIRPNDOCVE
Care or guardianship exercised by a deity

RETALIATION = 7. IIRTTOLNAAE
Revenge; getting even

SCANTY = 8. NYTCAS
Less than is needed

SUNDERED = 9. DESURNED
Separated

MANIFESTATION = 10. NSMTNOIAIFTEA
Expression; revelation; display

INCOHERENT = 11. HEORICNTEN
Rambling; confused; disjointed

ANNIHILATE = 12. IILETNHANA
Destroy

BENEVOLENCE = 13. LVBEONEECNE
Kindness; compassion; good will

COMMENSURATE = 14. ACTSEUORMMEN
Equal

CONSUMMATE = 15. MSANUOETMC
Complete

DENUNCIATION = 16. UOIAENCINNTD
Condemnation; criticism

EMANCIPATION = 17. TAANOPICNIME
Setting free

EXCULPATE = 18. LEPXTAEUC
To free from blame

IMPERTINENT = 19. INPTMRIEENT
Rude; disrespectful

VINDICATION = 20. AINNDICOTIV
Support; justification

180

_____   = 1. GITAADTE
Anxious; nervous

_____   = 2. AIMXM
Saying; a truth

_____   = 3. RDISMYA
Huge numbers

_____   = 4. NRODCEPEIV
Care or guardianship exercised by a deity

_____   = 5. QEILDAU
Drew back in fear

_____   = 6. TURAEPR
Delight; joy

_____   = 7. SAIATCYG
Wisdom

_____   = 8. TANCYS
Less than is needed

_____   = 9. HNAISGTC
Scornful; mocking

_____   = 10. NELIIFD
A person without belief in the religion of the writer

_____   = 11. NUECMPEDI
Rude behavior

_____   = 12. ITNTHAECU
Genuine; real

_____   = 13. LIAADEV
Made useful; helped

_____   = 14. NSERUDCE
Severely criticized

_____   = 15. UJEEORCTNC
Guessing

_____   = 16. IELFDED
Having one's good name ruined

_____   = 17. ETLDEASO
Deserted; uninhabited

_____   = 18. ERETXDOH
Urged; insisted

_____   = 19. MBUEI
Fill

_____   = 20. GNAICVLIE
Care; watchfulness

VOCABULARY JUGGLE LETTERS 2 ANSWER KEY *Narrative of the Life of Frederick Douglass*

AGITATED = 1. GITAADTE
Anxious; nervous

MAXIM = 2. AIMXM
Saying; a truth

MYRIADS = 3. RDISMYA
Huge numbers

PROVIDENCE = 4. NRODCEPEIV
Care or guardianship exercised by a deity

QUAILED = 5. QEILDAU
Drew back in fear

RAPTURE = 6. TURAEPR
Delight; joy

SAGACITY = 7. SAIATCYG
Wisdom

SCANTY = 8. TANCYS
Less than is needed

SCATHING = 9. HNAISGTC
Scornful; mocking

INFIDEL = 10. NELIIFD
A person without belief in the religion of the writer

IMPUDENCE = 11. NUECMPEDI
Rude behavior

AUTHENTIC = 12. ITNTHAECU
Genuine; real

AVAILED = 13. LIAADEV
Made useful; helped

CENSURED = 14. NSERUDCE
Severely criticized

CONJECTURE = 15. UJEEORCTNC
Guessing

DEFILED = 16. IELFDED
Having one's good name ruined

DESOLATE = 17. ETLDEASO
Deserted; uninhabited

EXHORTED = 18. ERETXDOH
Urged; insisted

IMBUE = 19. MBUEI
Fill

VIGILANCE = 20. GNAICVLIE
Care; watchfulness